ENGLISH - THAI

The only language book you ever need...

New version !

ENGLISH - THAI

2nd Edition 2002

Text by

Georg Gensbichler

Sarika Puangsombat, Yupin Puangsombat

Illustrations by

BanDon

ISBN 974 - 272 - 222 - 6

Published by

HOT & SPICY CO., LTD.

Internet: www.hotspicy.co.th

E-mail: mail@hotspicy.co.th

Fax Thailand: (66) - 2 - 914 1425

Fax USA: (1) - 209 - 671 7536

Printed in Thailand

ENGLISH - THAI

The only language book you ever need...

No time to study ?

Check our holiday & paperback versions !

New version !

CONTENTS

Check out our other books !

Available everywhere in Thailand or order online at

www.hotspicy.co.th

THAI LANGUAGE

This vastly extended version of our very popular English - Thai language guide books tries to explain common expressions and phrases as well as slang words you most probably will come along if you stay for a longer period in Thailand. The new (and important...) chapter about LOVE has been added to help you in all aspects of your visit. The chapter about FOOD has been greatly extended and we hope you will enjoy your culinary adventures in this beautiful country. If you are a first time tourist, a regular visitor or a longtime resident, we hope this book will help you with the sometimes confusing Thai language. We wish you all the best.

But it is very important to learn the correct pronunciation and use of tones from a Thai, otherwise you won't be understood.
Each Thai word can have 5 different meanings if different tones are used.
But note: not all words use all 5 tones.

Introduction to the 5 different tones:

1. middle tone: *common tone, pronounced flat.*
without symbol — *All syllables without symbol should be pronounced flat in this book.*

e.g.: ***maa*** = ***come*** มา

2. low tone: *similar to middle tone voice drops lower than normal*
symbol: ↓

e.g.: ***mai*** (↓) = ***new*** ใหม่

3. falling tone: *pronounced falling like an emphatic pronunciation in English*
symbol: ᴖ

e.g.: ***mai*** = ***not*** ไม่

4. high tone: *usually the most difficult.*
voice goes up higher than normal

symbol: *e.g.:* **maa** = **horse** ม้า

5. rising tone: *like the English question tone*

symbol: *e.g.:* **maa** = **dog** หมา

Polite syllables

*Whenever you speak Thai you should use the syllable **'khrap'** or **'kha'** at the end of the sentence.*
*If you are male you use **'khrap'** and if you are female you use **'kha'** at the end of each sentence.*
This particle was sometimes omitted in this book. However, you should always use this particle if you are not sure of it. Eventually you will get a feeling for the usage of this particle.

The Thai alphabet

Following a list of all 44 consonants and 32 vowels of the Thai alphabet.

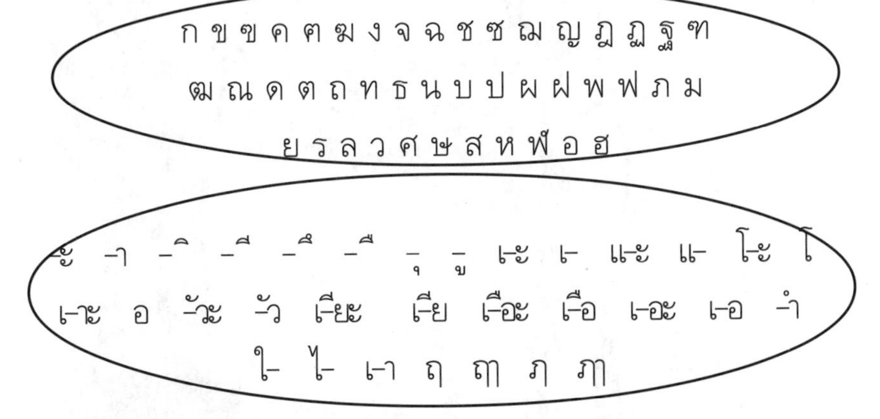

The vowels can be positioned before, after, above or under the consonants. However we do not want to discuss the writing of the Thai language in this book more extensively.

Good Morning !
Good Afternoon !
Good Evening !

Sawatdee khrap (kha) ! สวัสดี ครับ (ค่ะ)

The greeting is always the same whether it is nighttime or daytime.

The Thai person will make a wai and smile to greet you.

I (male)	**phom**	**ผม**
I (female)	**di chan, chan**	**ดิฉัน,ฉัน**
you	khun	คุณ
he, she	khao	เขา
it	man	มัน
we	(puag)rao	พวกเรา
you	(puag)khun	พวกคุณ
they	(puag)khao	พวกเขา
mine, my	khoong phom	ของผม
mine, my	khoong chan	ของฉัน
yours	khoong khun	ของคุณ
his, her	khoong khao	ของเขา
our	khoong puagrao	ของพวกเรา
yours	khoong puagkhun	ของพวกคุณ
theirs	khoong puagkhao	ของพวกเขา

Greetings - First Words

In the Thai language, you have to distinguish between female and male speaker. There are 17 different words for ***"I"*** *and many more for the other pronouns!*
Everything depends on the social status of the person to whom one talks. Following the most important words:

I for the male speaker:

phom	ผม	This is the most common expression.
graphom	กระผม	respectful, humble, used with telephone conversations
chan	ฉัน	between very good friends
gan	กัน	colloquial, man to man (friends)
atama	อาตมา	used by monks
kha pha chao	ข้าพเจ้า	for documents, at ministries, etc.
nicknames		not so common, mostly used by female speakers

I for the female speaker:

di chan	ดิฉัน	This is the most common expression.
chan	ฉัน	informal, between good friends
nuu	หนู	respectful, young person to elder person
dian	เดี้ยน	older women with high social status
nicknames		used very frequently

YOU:

khun (+ name)	คุณ	This is the most common expression.
tan	ท่าน	respectful, very polite, always to civil servants
toe	เธอ	only to a woman, between very good friends
phee...(+ name)	พี่	between friends
lung	ลุง	to elder men
paa, naa	ป้า, น้า	to elder women
khun naai	คุณนาย	only to women, meaning of 'madam'
nicknames		used frequently

mostly to domestic servants

First examples...

Welcome to Thailand !

Yindee ton rap !
ยินดีต้อนรับ

How are you ?

Sabaai dee mai khrap ?
สบายดีไหมครับ

Thanks, fine.

Sabaai dee khrap.
สบายดีครับ

What is your name ?

Khun chue arai khrap ?
คุณชื่ออะไรครับ

My name is...

Phom chue...
ผมชื่อ...

I am glad to meet you.

Yindee thee ruu chak.
ยินดีที่รู้จัก

I am happy to be able to meet you.

Phom dee jai thee daai phop khun.
ผมดีใจที่ได้พบคุณ

How old are you ?

Khun aayu thaorai khrap ?
คุณอายุเท่าไรครับ

Do you have a girlfriend / boyfriend ?

Khun mee faen laew rue yang ?
คุณมีแฟนหรือยัง

You will be asked this many times!

Are you married ?

Khun taeng ngaan laew rue yang ?
คุณแต่งงานแล้วหรือยัง

Do you remember me ?

Khun cham phom daai mai khrap ?
คุณจำผมได้ไหมครับ

Do you remember my name ?

Khun cham chue phom daai mai khrap ?
คุณจำชื่อผมได้ไหมครับ

Did we meet before ?

Khun kooi phop phom mai khrap ?
คุณเคยพบผมไหมครับ

I think we never met.

Phom khit waa mai kooi phop khun maa gawn.
ผมคิดว่าไม่เคยพบคุณมาก่อน

I can't remember.

Phom cham mai daai.
ผมจำไม่ได้

I forgot this already.

Phom luem laew.
ผมลืมแล้ว

I don't know.

Phom mai saap. Phom mai ruu chak.
ผมไม่ทราบ ผมไม่รู้จัก

I don't understand.

Phom mai khao jai.
ผมไม่เข้าใจ

Please speak more slowly !

Chuai phoot chaa chaa nooi !
ช่วยพูดช้าๆหน่อย

Please speak louder !

Chuai phoot dung dung nooi !
ช่วยพูดดังๆหน่อย

Please say again !

Chuai phoot eek khrung !
ช่วยพูดอีกครั้ง

How do you call this in Thai ?

Nee phaasaa Thai riiak waa arai ?
นี่ภาษาไทยเรียกว่าอะไร

Do I pronounce it correctly ?

Phom ook siiang thook mai khrap ?
ผมออกเสียงถูกไหมครับ

What do you work ?

Khun tham ngaan arai khrap ?
คุณทำงานอะไรครับ

Where do you work ?

Khun tham ngaan theenai khrap ?
คุณทำงานที่ไหนครับ

Where do you live ?

Khun yuu theenai khrap ?
คุณอยู่ที่ไหนครับ

I live not far from here.

Phom yuu glai glai thee nee.
ผมอยู่ใกล้ๆที่นี่

Can I bring you home ?

Phom song khun thee baan daai mai khrap ?
ผมไปส่งคุณที่บ้านได้ไหมครับ

Can I ask you something ?

Phom kho thaam arai nooi khrap ?
ผมขอถามอะไรหน่อยครับ

Please come in !

Choen kaang nai khrap ! Choen khao maa loi khrap !
เชิญข้างในครับ เชิญเข้ามาเลยครับ

Please sit down !

Choen nang khrap !
เชิญนั่งครับ

Would you like to have tea or coffee ?

Khun yaak duem chaa rue kaafae khrap ?
คุยอยากดื่มชาหรือกาแฟครับ

A glass of water please !

Kho naam yen nooi khrap !
ขอน้ำเย็นหน่อยครับ

I have to go now !

Phom tawng pai diaw nee !
ผมต้องไปเดี๋ยวนี้

I have to go to my office (company).

Phom tawng pai borisat.
ผมต้องไปบริษัท

Bye bye.

Laa goon.
ลาก่อน

See you tomorrow.

Phrung nee phop gan.
พรุ่งนี้พบกัน

See you later.

Laew phop gan na.
แล้วพบกันนะ

See you soon.

Laew phop gan mai.
แล้วพบกันใหม่

Good luck !

Chook dee na !
โชคดีนะ

My regards to..

Faak kwaam khit thueng...
ฝากความคิดถึง...

Thank you.

Khawp khun khrap.
ขอบคุณครับ

English - Thai - All you have to know

Available as pocket book

P a p e r b a c k

VERBS

What you always hear...

ask	thaam	ถาม
be	pen	เป็น
be (located)	yuu	อยู่
buy	sue	ซื้อ
can, be able	daai	ได้
carry	tue *(things)*	ถือ
carry	um *(persons)*	อุ้ม
come	maa	มา
do, make	tham	ทำ
drink	duem	ดื่ม
eat	kin (thaan) kaao	กินข้าว,ทานข้าว
find	phop	พบ
forget	luem	ลืม
give	haai	ให้
go	pai	ไป
go out	pai thiaw	ไปเที่ยว
have	mee	มี
hear	daai yin	ได้ยิน
help	chuai	ช่วย
know	ruu chak	รู้จัก
laugh	hua raw	หัวเราะ
like	chawp	ชอบ
live, reside	yuu	อยู่
look	duu, mawng	ดู, มอง
look for, search	haa	หา
love	ruk	รัก

must	tawng	ต้อง
need, want	tawng gaan	ต้องการ
pay	chaai ngoen	จ่ายเงิน
play	len	เล่น
read	aan	อ่าน
remember	jam	จำ
see	hen	เห็น
sell	khaai	ขาย
sit	nang	นั่ง
sleep	nawn	นอน
smile	yim	ยิ้ม
speak	phoot	พูด
swim	wai naam	ว่ายน้ำ
take	aw	เอา
tell	bawk	บอก
understand	khao jai	เข้าใจ
wait	roo	รอ
want	yaak	อยาก
wash, launder	sak	ซัก
wash, shampoo	sa	สระ
wash, clean	laang	ล้าง
work	tham ngaan	ทำงาน
write	khian	เขียน

sak phaa = *wash clothes* ซักผ้า
sa phom = *shampoo one's hair* สระผม
laang mue = *wash one's hands* ล้างมือ

Additional verbs

AAA

accompany	song	ส่ง
add up	buag	บวก
advertise	tham khoosanaa	ทำโฆษณา
agree	hen duai	เห็นด้วย
announce	pragaat	ประกาศ
answer	toop	ช่วยเหลือ
arrive	maa thueng	มาถึง
assist, help	chuai luea	ตอบ
assume	sommut	สมมติ
attack	choom tee	โจมตี

BBB

begin, start	roem	เริ่ม
believe	chuea	เชื่อ
bet	panan	พนัน
blossom	baan	บาน
borrow	khoo yuem	ขอยืม
break	hag	หัก
build	saang	สร้าง

CCC

call (phone)	to pai haa	โทรไปหา
cancel	yok loek	ยกเลิก
celebrate	chaloong	ฉลอง
change	plian	เปลี่ยน
chase away	lai, lai pai	ไล่, ไล่ไป

check, examine	truat	ตรวจ
climb	peen	ปีน
close	pit	ปิด
collect	sasoom	สะสม
command	sang	สั่ง
complain	bon	บ่น
convince	tham hai chuea man	ทำให้เชื่อมั่น
cook	tham kap kaao	ทำกับข้าว
correct	gaekai	แก้ไข
count	naap lek	นับเลข
cry	roong haai	ร้องให้
cut	tat	ตัด

DDD

dance	tenram	เต้นรำ
deliver	faak	ฝาก
deliver	song haai	ส่งให้
dig	kut	ขุด
discover	kon phop	ค้นพบ
divide	haan	หาร
dream	faan	ฝัน
dust	pat fun	ปัดฝุ่น

EEE

end, finish	loek	เลิก
escape, flee	nee	หนี
explain	athibaai	อธิบาย
export	song ook	ส่งออก

FFF

feed	haai aahaan	ให้อาหาร
feel	ruusuek	รู้สึก
find	phop	พบ
flirt	lao lom	เล้าโลม
follow	tit tham	ติดตาม
forecast, predict	tham naai	ทำนาย
fry	thoot	ทอด

GGG

gain (weight)	poem nam nak	เพิ่มน้ำหนัก
gather, assemble	ruam gan	ร่วมกัน
get up	tuen	ตื่น
give	yok haai	ยกให้
go down(stairs)	long bandai	ลงบันได
go for a walk	doen len	เดินเล่น
go up(stairs)	khuen bandai	ขึ้นบันได
grow	pluug	ปลูก

HHH

hang	kwaen	แขวน
happen	goet	เกิด
hate	gleeat	เกลียด
hide	son	ซ่อน
hit	tee	ตี
hope	wang	หวัง
hunt	laa	ล่า

I I I, JJJ

ice-skate	len saket	เล่นสเก็ต
import	nam khaao	นำเข้า
interrupt	kat chang waa	ขัดจังหวะ
invent	pratit	ประดิษฐ์
invite	chuan	ชวน
joke	phoot talog	พูดตลก
jump	gratoot	กระโดด

KKK

kick	te	เตะ
kiss	hom	หอม
kiss (on the cheeks)	choob	จูบ
knock (ring the bell)	got grating	กดกระดิ่ง
knock (on the door)	khoo pratuu	เคาะประตู

LLL

leave, abandon	ook chaak	ออกจาก
lend	haai yuem	ให้ยืม
let, lease, rent out	haai chao	ให้เช่า
lie	goohok	โกหก
listen	fang	ฟัง
look after,take care	fao	เฝ้า
lose	pae	แพ้

MMM

manage	chat gaan	จัดการ
marry	taeng ngaan	แต่งงาน
misunderstand	khao chai phit	เข้าใจผิด

mow	tat yaa	ตัดหญ้า
multiply	koon	คูณ

NNN

need, require	chaai	จ่าย

OOO

open	poet	เปิด
order	sang	สั่ง

PPP

paint	taa see	ทาสี
pay	kep ngoen	เก็บเงิน
persuade	chak chuan	ชักชวน
pick up, come for	rap	รับ
pick up, lift	yok, kep	ยก, เก็บ
plough, plow	tai naa	ไถนา
point to	shee	ชี้
pour	tae	เท
prevent	poong gan	ป้องกัน
produce	phalit	ผลิต
pull	dueng	ดึง
punch	tooi	ต่อย
punish	long toot	ลงโทษ
push	plak	ผลัก

QQQ

quarrel	talo	ทะเลาะ

RRR

receive	daai rap	ได้รับ
register	long thabian	ลงทะเบียน
remove,clear away	kep khong	เก็บของ
renew	too aayoo	ต่ออายุ
rent, lease	chao	เช่า
repair	som	ซ่อม
respect	khaorop	เคารพ
rest	phak, phak nueai	พัก, พักเหนื่อย
run	wing	วิ่ง

SSS

send	song	ส่ง
shoot	ying	ยิง
shout	tagoon	ตะโกน
sing	roong plaeng	ร้องเพลง
slimming	lot nam nak	ลดน้ำหนัก
smell	domglin	ดมกลิ่น
smoke	soob buree	สูบบุหรี่
spell	sa got	สะกด
stand	yuen	ยืน
start, begin	roem	เริ่ม
stitch, sew	yep	เย็บ
subtract	lop	ลบ
suggest	sanoe	เสนอ
suppose, guess	songsai	สงสัย

TTT

take a ride	kap rot len	ขับรถเล่น
taste	chim	ชิม
teach	soon	สอน
think	khit	คิด
throw	paa, yon	ปา, โยน
touch, grab	chap	จับ
translate	plae	แปล
travel	doenthaang	เดินทาง
try	paiayam	พยายาม
try, attempt	paiayam, long	พยายาม, ลอง

VVV

vaccuum, hoover	toot fun	ดูดฝุ่น
visit	pai haa, yiamyian	ไปหา, เยี่ยมเยียน

WWW

wake up	plug	ปลุก
walk	doen	เดิน
waste	sia	เสีย
whisper	grasip	กระซิบ
win	chana	ชนะ
wipe	chet	เช็ด
work on, deal with	treeam	เตรียม

ADJECTIVES

big	**yai**	**ใหญ่**
small	**lek**	**เล็ก**
cheap	thook	ถูก
expensive	phaeng	แพง
clean	**sa aat**	**สะอาด**
dirty	**sokgaprok**	**สกปรก**
dangerous	antaraai	อันตราย
safe	ploot phai	ปลอดภัย
dark	**muet**	**มืด**
light	**sawaang**	**สว่าง**
easy	ngaii	ง่าย
difficult	yaak	ยาก
empty	**waang, plaao**	**ว่าง, เปล่า**
full	**tem**	**เต็ม**
fat	oo-un	อ้วน
thin, slim	phawm	ผอม
thick	**naa**	**หนา**
thin	**bang**	**บาง**
good	dee	ดี
bad	lae-aw	เลว
hard	**khaeng**	**แข็ง**
soft	**noom / oon**	**นุ่ม / อ่อน**
hot	rawn	ร้อน
cold	naao / yen	หนาว/เย็น

*Be careful with **naao** or **yen**.*
***yen** can be translated with **cool** or **chilly** (weather) and **naao** means **cold**.*
*However: **'naam yen'** = cold water* น้ำเย็น

illegal	**pit got maai**	**ผิดกฎหมาย**
legal	**thook got maai**	**ถูกกฎหมาย**
light	bao	เบา
heavy	nak	หนัก
little	**noi**	**น้อย**
a lot, plenty	**maak**	**มาก**
loud	dung	ดัง
quiet	baw	เบา
near	**glai**	**ใกล้**
far	**glai**	**ไกล**
old	gaw	เก่า
new	mai	ใหม่
old	**gae**	**แก่**
young (girl)	**saao**	**สาว**
young (boy)	**num**	**หนุ่ม**
ordinary	thammadaa	ธรรมดา
special	peeset	พิเศษ
poor	**chon**	**จน**
rich	**ruai**	**รวย**
ripe	suk	สุก
unripe	dip	ดิบ
shallow	**tuen**	**ตื้น**
deep	**lueg**	**ลึก**
short	san	สั้น
long	naan	นาน
short	**san**	**สั้น**
long	**yaao**	**ยาว**

Be careful with the pronunciation!

silly	ngo	โง่
clever	chalaad	ฉลาด
skilful	**keng**	**เก่ง**
clumsy	**ngoom ngaam**	**งุ่มง่าม**
slow	chaa	ช้า
quick	rae-o	เร็ว
tidy, neat	**riap rooi**	**เรียบร้อย**
untidy	**loe thoe**	**เลอะเทอะ**
ugly	kee-re	ขี้เหร่
beautiful	suai	สวย
weak	**oon ae**	**อ่อนแอ**
strong	**khaeng raeng**	**แข็งแรง**
wide	kwang	กว้าง
narrow	khaep	แคบ
wet	**piak**	**เปียก**
try	**haeng**	**แห้ง**
wrong	pit	ผิด
right	thook	ถูก

Others

famous	mee chue siiang	มีชื่อเสียง
important	samkan	สำคัญ
necessary	champen	จำเป็น
popular	pen thee nee yom	เป็นที่นิยม
similar	klaai	คล้าย
useful	mee prayot	มีประโยชน์

'mai koi dee' *= not so good* ไม่ค่อยดี
'mai dee loi' *= not good at all* ไม่ดีเลย
'mai...loi' *= not at all* ไม่...เลย

'mai laeo' *= not bad* ไม่เลว
'laeo maak' *= very bad* เลวมาก

'suan' *= part* ส่วน
'baang suan' *= a few* บางส่วน
'suan nooi' *= the least* ส่วนน้อย
'suan maak' *= the most* ส่วนมาก
'suan tua' *= personal* ส่วนตัว
'suan chaliia' *= average* ส่วนเฉลี่ย
'suan tiaw' *= individual(ly)* ส่วนเดียว
'suan baeng' *= share* ส่วนแบ่ง

QUESTION and ANSWER

Questions words

There are two ways to form a question:
1. use any of the listed question words
or
*2. add the word **'mai'** at the end of the sentence*

How ?	yaang ngai	อย่างไหน
How far ?	glai thaorai	ไกลเท่าไร
How many ?	kee	กี่
How much ?	thaorai	เท่าไร
What ?	arai	อะไร
When ?	mue-arai	เมื่อไร
Why ?	thammai	ทำไม
Where ?	theenai	ที่ไหน
Where from ?	chaak nai	จากไหน
Where to ?	(pai) nai	(ไป) ไหน
Which ?	(an) nai	(อัน) ไหน
Which way ?	thang nai	ทางไหน
Who ?	khrai	ใคร
Who ?	(khon) nai	(คน) ไหน

*To form a question without question word, just add the word '**mai**' to the end of the sentence.*

Can you speak Thai ?

Khun phoot phaasaa thai daai **mai** ?
คุณพูดภาษาไทยได้ไหม

Examples: questions

When will you come back again ?

Khun cha glap maa mue-arai ?
คุณจะกลับมาเมื่อไร

Why don't you have a girlfriend ?

Thammai khun mai mee faen ?
ทำไมคุณไม่มีแฟน

Thammai (=why) *can be placed at the beginning or end of the question. However, certain questions ending with 'thammai' could be offensive!*

What do you work ?

Khun tham ngaan arai ?
คุณทำงานอะไร

Who (which person) can speak Thai ?

Khon nai phoot phaasaa thai daai ?
คนไหนพูดภาษาไทยได้

Who can speak Thai ?

Khrai phoot phaasaa thai daai ?
ใครพูดภาษาไทยได้

Which sunglasses do you like ?

Khun chawp waentaa an nai ?
คุณชอบแว่นตาอันไหน

How far is it to the market ?

Talaat glai thaorai chaak theenee ?
ตลาดไกลเท่าไรจากที่นี่

How do you do that ?

Nee tham yaang ngai ?
นี่ทำอย่างไง

How much is it ?

Raakhaa thaorai ?
ราคาเท่าไร

How many siblings do you have ?

Khun mee peenong kee khon ?
คุณมีพี่น้องกี่คน

Be careful: Always use a classification after the word ***kee (=how many)!***

Where do you live ?

Khun phak yuu theenai ?
คุณพักอยู่ที่ไหน

Where do you come from ?

Khun maa chaak nai ?
คุณมาจากไหน

Where do you go?

Khun pai nai ?
คุณไปไหน

Which is the way to the market ?

Thang nai pai talaat ?
ทางไหนไปสนามบิน

YES and NO

1) There is no easy answer for ***YES*** *or* ***NO*** *in the Thai language. All depends on the asked question.*

Yes --- No

Just repeat the verb of the question to say ***YES***

Add the particle ***'mai' (=not)*** *in front of the verb of the question to say* ***NO***

2) Many times the question will end with the particle

'...chai mai' (= isn't it?)

The answer with ***'chai'*** *means* ***YES*** *and* ***'mai chai'*** *means* ***NO****.*

yes	**chai**	ใช่
no	**mai chai**	ไม่ใช่

3) You can also use the particle ***'khrap'*** *or* ***'kha'*** *for* ***YES*** *and* ***'mai khrap'*** *or* ***'mai kha'*** *for* ***NO****.*

yes	**khrap / kha**	ครับ / ค่ะ
no	**mai khrap / mai kha**	ไม่ครับ / ไม่ค่ะ

Thank you	khawp khun	ขอบคุณ
No, thank you	mai aw khawp khun	ไม่เอาขอบคุณ
Please	karunaa	กรุณา

Additional words

question	kham thaam	คำถาม
answer	kham toob	คำตอบ
already	laew	แล้ว
also, too	duai	ด้วย
although	yaang rai go dee	อย่างไรก็ดี
and	lae	และ
and then	laew go	แล้วก็
because	phro waa	เพราะว่า
but	tae	แต่
if, when	taa	ถ้า
in case of	puea waa	เผื่อว่า
maybe, perhaps	aat cha	อาจจะ
nevertheless	mae waa	แม้ว่า
only	thaonan	เท่านั้น
or	rue	หรือ
or not yet?	laew rue yang	แล้วหรือยัง
or not yet?	laew rue plao	แล้วหรือเปล่า
possibly	khong cha	คงจะ
with	gap	กับ
yet	yang	ยัง,
not yet	yang mai	ยังไม่

NUMBERS and COUNTING

๐	0	soon	ศูนย์
๑	1	nueng	หนึ่ง
๒	2	sawng	สอง
๓	3	saam	สาม
๔	4	see	สี่
๕	5	haa	ห้า
๖	6	hok	หก
๗	7	chaet	เจ็ด
๘	8	paet	แปด
๙	9	gaao	เก้า
๑๐	10	sip	สิบ
๑๑	11	sip-at	สิบเอ็ด
๑๒	12	sip-sawng	สิบสอง
๒๐	20	yee-sip	ยี่สิบ
๒๑	21	yee-sip-at	ยี่สิบเอ็ด
๓๐	30	saam-sip	สามสิบ
๑๐๐	100	nueng rooi	หนึ่งร้อย
๓๒๕	325	saam rooi yee-sip-haa	สามร้อยยี่สิบห้า
๑๐๐๐	1.000	nueng phun	หนึ่งพัน
๑๐๐๐๐	10.000	nueng meun	หนึ่งหมื่น
๑๐๐๐๐๐	100.000	nueng saen	หนึ่งแสน
๑๐๐๐๐๐๐	1,000.000	nueng laan	หนึ่งล้าน

dozen	law	โหล
pair	kuu	คู่
2 times, 5 times, etc.	2 khrung, 5 khrung	ครั้ง
first time	khrung raek	ครั้งแรก
last time	khrung sut taai	ครั้งสุดท้าย

Counting

To count things or people in the Thai language, you have to use special words, particles (classification).
You just add this particle to the word.

There are about 80 different particles!

particle for :	***particle, classification***	
cars	khan	คัน
trees	ton	ต้น
flowers, joss sticks	dok	ดอก
letters, newspapers	chabap	ฉบับ
stamps, stars	duang	ดวง
books, candles, knives	lem	เล่ม
eggs	fong	ฟอง
elect. appliances (TV, radio)	khrueang	เครื่อง
ships, airplanes	lam	ลำ
fruits	look	ลูก
necklaces	sen	เส้น
houses, closet, cupboard	lang	หลัง
dress, suit	chut	ชุด
small things	**an**	อัน
Royal persons	ong	องค์
people	**khon**	คน
monks	roop	รูป
glasses, dishes, photos	met	เม็ด
rolls (film, toilet paper)	muan	ม้วน
pieces (cake, dress)	chin	ชิ้น
glasses, plates, photos	bai	ใบ

particle for :	*particle, classification*	
animals, clothes, furniture	tua	ตัว
carpets	puen	ผืน
clocks, watches	ruean	เรือน
teeth	see	ซี่
cigarettes, cigars	muan	มวน

Examples: Counting

2 children	look soong khon *(child - 2 - classification)*	ลูกสองคน
3 cars	rot saam khan *(car - 3 - classification)*	รถสามคัน

*If you can't remember the correct particle, you can use the word **'an'**.*

Miscellaneous

other, others	uen	อื่น
that	nan	นั่น
the same	muean	เหมือน
every, each	tuk	ทุก

TIME

To tell the time, the Thai language divides one day into 4 x 6 hours. This is the traditional way and is still used today. However, you will also hear the International way of telling the time (24 hours) or a mixture of both.

'thee ': *night time*

0:00	thi-ang khuen	เที่ยงคืน
1:00	thee nueng	ตีหนึ่ง
2:00	thee sawng	ตีสอง
3:00	thee saam	ตีสาม
4:00	thee see	ตีสี่
5:00	thee haa	ตีห้า

'mawng chaao': *morning*

6:00	hok mawng chaao	หกโมงเช้า
7:00	nueng mawng chaao	หนึ่งโมงเช้า
8:00	sawng mawng chaao	สองโมงเช้า
9:00	saam mawng chaao	สามโมงเช้า
10:00	see mawng chaao	สี่โมงเช้า
11:00	haa mawng chaao	ห้าโมงเช้า

'baai mawng': *afternoon*

12:00	thi-ang wun	เที่ยงวัน
13:00	baai (nueng) mawng	บ่าย(หนึ่ง)โมง
14:00	baai sawng mawng	บ่ายสองโมง
15:00	baai saam mawng	บ่ายสามโมง
16:00	baai see mawng	บ่ายสี่โมง
17:00	baai haa mawng	บ่ายห้าโมง

***'thoom'**: evening*

18:00	hok mawng yaen	หกโมงเย็น
19:00	nueng thoom	หนึ่งทุ่ม
20:00	sawng thoom	สองทุ่ม
21:00	saam thoom	สามทุ่ม
22:00	see thoom	สี่ทุ่ม
23:00	haa thoom	ห้าทุ่ม
14:30	baai sawng mawng khrueng	บ่ายสองโมงครึ่ง
14.50	eek sip naathee baai saam mawng	อีกสิบนาทีบ่ายสามโมง

Be careful:
9 o'clock in the morning **(= 3 mawng chaao)**
3 o'clock in the afternoon **(= baai 3 mawng)**
9 o'clock in the evening **(= 3 thoom)**

What is the time?	Kee mawng lae-u	กี่โมงแล้ว
time	waelaa	เวลา
hour	chua mawng	ชั่วโมง
half hour	khrueng chua mawng	ครึ่งชั่วโมง
minute	naathee	นาที
second	winaathee	วินาที
watch, clock	naaligaa	นาฬิกา
alarm clock	naaliga plug	นาฬิกาปลุก

Additional words

after, when	lang chaak	หลังจาก
always	samoe, talawt pai	เสมอ, ตลอดไป
appointment, date	mee nut	มีนัด
approximate	pramaan	ประมาณ
at, on	thee	ที่
before, ago	thee lae-u	ที่แล้ว
before, previous	gawn	ก่อน
be late	maa chaa, maa saai	มาช้า,มาสาย
coincidence, accidental	doi bang oen	โดยบังเอิญ
constant, permanent	talawt waelaa	ตลอดเวลา
ever	khoei	เคย
in, still	eek	อีก
in this moment	kumlang	กำลัง
in time	tan waelaa	ทันเวลา
just	phoeng, muea kee	เพิ่ง, เมื่อกี้
just now, now	diaw nee, toon nee	เดี๋ยวนี้, ตอนนี้
last	thee lae-u	ที่แล้ว
meeting	nut phop	นัดพบ
nearly, almost	gueab cha	เกือบจะ
next	naa	หน้า
normally	pogadtee	ปกติ
nowadays	patchuban	ปัจจุบัน
on time	trong waelaa	ตรงเวลา
schedule	gamnot waelaa	กำหนดเวลา
since	tangtae	ตั้งแต่

sleep early	hua kam	หัวค่ำ
sometimes	baang khrung	บางครั้ง
soon	rae-o rae-o nee	เร็วๆนี้
urgent	reeb	รีบ
wake up early	tuen chaao	ตื่นเช้า
waste of time	sia weelaa	เสียเวลา

Examples: time

Sorry for being late !

Khaw thawt thee maa chaa !
ขอโทษที่มาช้า

Sorry for let you waiting !

Khaw thawt thee tham haai khun raw !
ขอโทษที่ทำให้คุณรอ

Sorry for disturbing you !

Khaw thawt thee rop guan khun !
ขอโทษที่รบกวนคุณ

Sorry, but I am busy !

Khaw thawt phom mee tooraa !
ขอโทษผมมีธุระ

You should come here on time !

Khun khuan cha maa theenee trong waelaa !
คุณควรจะมาที่นี่ตรงเวลา

How long more ?

Mee waelaa eek thaorai ?
มีเวลาอีกเท่าไหร่

Time is up !

Mot waelaa !
หมดเวลา

Time to go.

Daai waelaa lae-u.
ได้เวลาแล้ว

I have to adjust my watch.

Phom tung waelaa.
ผมตั้งเวลา

My watch is 3 minutes fast.

Naaligaa phom rae-o pai saam naathee.
นาฬิกาผมเร็วไปสามนาที

My wach is 3 minutes late.

Naaligaa phom chaa pai saam naathee.
นาฬิกาผมช้าไปสามนาที

My watch goes exactly.

Naaligaa phom trong waelaa.
นาฬิกาผมตรงเวลา

My watch stopped working.

Naaligaa taai.
นาฬิกาตาย

Do you have time ?

Do you have time ?

Waang mai ? Mee waelaa mai ?
ว่างไหม, มีเวลาไหม

About when ?

Toon nai ? Pramaan kee mawng ?
ตอนไหน, ประมาณกี่โมง

Is that too early ?

Rae-o goen pai rue plaao ?
เร็วเกินไปหรือเปล่า

When is it okay ?

Khun saduak mue-arai ?
คุณสะดวกเมื่อไหร่

When can I meet you ?

Cha phop khun daai mue-arai ?
จะพบคุณได้เมื่อไหร่

Whenever.

Mue-arai go daai.
เมื่อไหร่ก็ได้

Always.

Talawt waelaa.
ตลอดเวลา

You say when it's best.

Khun waang mue-arai bawk phom.
คุณว่างเมื่อไหร่บอกผม

I have no time.

Mai waang. Kamlang yoong.
ไม่ว่างกำลังยุ่ง

That's a bad day for me.

Wun nun mai waang.
วันนั้นไม่ว่าง

This day is okay.

Wun nun go daai.
วันนั้นก็ได้

Come later.

Diaw maa.
เดี๋ยวมา

Come again.

Maa eek na.
มาอีกนะ

Can you come ?

Maa daai mai ?
มาได้ไหม

I think I can come.

Phom khit waa pai daai.
ผมคิดว่าไปได้

How long are you in Thailand already ?

Khun yuu mue-ang Thai naan thaorai lae-u ?
คุณอยู่เมืองไทยนานเท่าไหร่แล้ว

When will you go ?

Cha pai kee mawng ?
จะไปกี่โมง

It depends.

Lae-u tae.
แล้วแต่

If I have fun, I will stay here.

Taa sanuk phom/chan cha yuu too.
ถ้าสนุกผม/ฉันจะอยู่ต่อ

If I am bored, I will go home.

Taa naa bue-a phom/chan go cha glup baan.
ถ้าน่าเบื่อผม/ฉันก็จะกลับบ้าน

What should we do now ?

Rao cha tham arai toon nee ?
เราจะทำอะไรตอนนี้

I want to stay longer.

Yaak yuu eek nooi.
อยากอยู่อีกหน่อย

See you soon.

Rao phop gan eek.
แล้วพบกันอีก

See you tomorrow.

Phrung nee phop gan.
พรุ่งนี้พบกัน

I will come back soon.

Phom/chan cha glup rae-o rae-o nee.
ผม/ฉันจะกลับเร็วๆนี้

Are you ready ?

Set laew rue yung ? Riap rooi laew rue yung ?
เสร็จแล้วหรือยัง, เรียบร้อยแล้วหรือยัง

Ready, right ?

Set laew chai mai ?
เสร็จแล้วใช่ไหม

Ready.

Set laew.
เสร็จแล้ว

Not yet.

Yung.
ยัง

Soon ready.

Diaw go set.
เดี๋ยวก็เสร็จ

One moment please !

Raw sak khroo !
รอสักครู่

Soon.

Rae-u rae-u nee. Paep diaw.
เร็วๆนี้, แป๊บเดียว

I am coming. Wait a moment.

Diaw phom/chan cha maa.
เดี๋ยวผม/ฉันจะมา

Not now. Wait a little bit.

Diaw gon. Karuna raw sak khroo.
เดี๋ยวก่อนกรุณารอสักครู่

I will go soon !

Diaw phom/chan cha pai !
เดี๋ยวผม/ฉันจะไป

The last time.

Mue-a gon.
เมื่อก่อน

Let's start !

Roem daai laew !
เริ่มได้แล้ว

Let's continue !

Tham to daai laew !
ทำต่อได้แล้ว

Do it later.

Aw wai thee lang.
เอาไว้ทีหลัง

In the next life.

Chaat naa.
ชาติหน้า

DATE

Days of the week

Monday	wun chan	วันจันทร์
Tuesday	wun ungkhaan	วันอังคาร
Wednesday	wun phoot	วันพุธ
Thursday	wun phuruehut	วันพฤหัส
Friday	wun suk	วันศุกร์
Saturday	wun sao	วันเสาร์
Sunday	wun aathit	วันอาทิตย์
today	wun nee	วันนี้
yesterday	mue-a waan nee	เมื่อวานนี้
tomorrow	phrung nee	พรุ่งนี้
after tomorrow	maruen nee	มะรืนนี้
before yesterday	mue-a waan suen	เมื่อวานซืน
morning	ton chaao	ตอนเช้า
afternoon	ton baai	ตอนบ่าย
evening	ton yen	ตอนเย็น
day / night	wun / khuen	วัน / คืน
this morning	chaao nee	เช้านี้
this afternoon	baai nee	บ่ายนี้
this evening	yen nee	เย็นนี้
every morning	tuk chaao	ทุกเช้า
in the evening	glaang khuen	กลางคืน
this night	khuen nee	คืนนี้
last night	khuen thee laew	คืนที่แล้ว

from Monday to Friday	wun chan thueng wun suk	วันจันทร์ถึงวันศุกร์
every other day	wun wen wun	วันเว้นวัน
the whole day	tang wun	ทั้งวัน
once a day	wun la khrung	วันละครั้ง
five days a week	haa wun too aathit	ห้าวันต่ออาทิตย์
during the day	nai ton glaang wun	ในตอนกลางวัน
weekend	soot sapdaa, sao-aathit	สุดสัปดาห์, เสาร์อาทิตย์
week	aathit	อาทิตย์

Months

All months with 30 days end with ***'yon'****.*
Month with 31 days end with ***'khom'****.*

January	makaraa khom	มกราคม
February	kumphaa phan	กุมภาพันธ์
March	meenaa khom	มีนาคม
April	maesaa yon	เมษายน
May	phruetsaphaa khom	พฤษภาคม
June	mithunaa yon	มิถุนายน
July	karakadaa khom	กรกฎาคม
August	singhaa khom	สิงหาคม
September	kanyaa yon	กันยายน
October	tulaa khom	ตุลาคม
November	phruetsadchigaa yon	พฤศจิกายน
December	thanwaa khom	ธันวาคม

month duean เดือน
beginning of month ton duean ต้นเดือน
end of month plai duean ปลายเดือน
this month duean nee เดือนนี้
next month duean naa เดือนหน้า
last month duean thee laew เดือนที่แล้ว

There are 3 seasons in Thailand:
***1) ruedoo rawn:** March - June*
***2) ruedoo fon:** July - October*
***3) ruedoo naao:** November - February*

season ruedoo ฤดู
hot season ruedoo rawn (naa rawn) ฤดูร้อน (หน้าร้อน)
rainy season ruedoo fon (naa fon) ฤดูฝน (หน้าฝน)
cool season ruedoo naao (naa naao) ฤดูหนาว (หน้าหนาว)

Comparison our seasons

spring ruedoo bai mai plee ฤดูใบไม้ผลิ
summer ruedoo rawn ฤดูร้อน
autumn ruedoo bai mai ruang ฤดูใบไม้ร่วง
winter ruedoo naao ฤดูหนาว

year pee ปี
century satawat ศตวรรษ
date wun thee วันที่

Date in Thai:
wun thee + number + month
for example : August 16th =
wun thee 16 (= sip hok) singhaa khom
วันที่ ๑๖ สิงหาคม

SHOPPING

Clothing

'sai sue-a' = *put on (clothes)* ใส่เสื้อ
'tot sue-a' = *take off (clothes)* ถอดเสื้อ
'taeng tua' = *dress nicely* แต่งตัว

clothes, clothing	sue-a phaa	เสื้อผ้า
material, fabric	phaa	ผ้า
bag	gra paao	กระเป๋า
belt	kemkut	เข็มขัด
blouse	sue-a	เสื้อ
dress	chut	ชุด
gloves	thoong mue	ถุงมือ
hat, cap	muag	หมวก
jacket	sue-a jacket	เสื้อแจ็กเก็ท
pyjamas	chut non	ชุดนอน
sandal	rong thaao tae	รองเท้าแตะ
shirt	sue-a	เสื้อ
shoe	rong thaao	รองเท้า
shorts	gaang gaeng kaa san	กางเกงขาสั้น
skirt	graprong	กระโปรง
sock	thoong thaao	ถุงเท้า
stockings	thoong nong	ถุงน่อง
suit	suit	สูท
sweater	sue-a naao	เสื้อหนาว
swim wear	chut wai naam	ชุดว่ายน้ำ

towel	phaa tschet tua	ผ้าเช็ดตัว
trouser	gaang gaeng	กางเกง
T-shirt	sue-a yuet	เสื้อยืด
underwear	gaang gaeng nai	กางเกงใน

Jewellery

bracelet	gamlai mue	กำไลมือ
necklace	sooi koo	สร้อยคอ
earring	tang hoo	ต่างหู
ring	waen	แหวน
gem stone	ploew	พลอย
diamond	phaet	เพชร
emerald	moraakot	มรกต
jade	yok	หยก
opal	muk daa	มุกดา
pearl	khai muk	ไข่มุก
ruby	tap tim	ทับทิม
sapphire	ploew see kraam, nin	พลอยสีคราม, นิล
gold	thong	ทอง
silver	ngoen	เงิน

Useful shopping words

antique, old	boraan	โบราณ
cotton	phaa faai	ผ้าฝ้าย
fake, forgery	plom plaeng	ปลอมแปลง
fashion	faeshon	แฟชั่น
hand-made	tham duai mue	ทำด้วยมือ
ladies wear	sue-a phaa sa tree	เสื้อผ้าสตรี
men's wear	sue-a phaa phoo rut	เสื้อผ้าบุรุษ
leather	nang sat	หนังสัตว์
made from...	tham duai	ทำด้วย
market	taalaat	ตลาด
nylon	phaa nailon	ผ้าไนล่อน
present	khoong kwaan	ของขวัญ
quality	kunapaap	คุณภาพ
refund	khuen ngoen haai	คืนเงินให้
sale	lot raakhaa	ลดราคา
shoe shop	raan khaai rong thaao	ร้านขายรองเท้า
silk	phaa mai	ผ้าไหม
Thai silk	phaa mai thai	ผ้าไหมไทย
special offer	lot peesaet	ลดพิเศษ
supermarket	supermaaket	ซุปเปอร์มาเก็ต
synthetic	phaa yai sang kro	ผ้าใยสังเคราะห์
tailor	raan tut sue-a	ร้านตัดเสื้อ
type, sort, kind	chanit	ชนิด
wool	phaa kon gae	ผ้าขนแกะ

Toilet articles

brush	praeng	แปรง
comb	wee	หวี
gel	gel sai phom	เจลใส่ผม
hair dye	naam yaa yom phom	น้ำยาใส่ผม
hair shampoo	yaa sa phom, shampoo	ยาสระผม, แชมพู
hairspray	saprae chit phom	สเปรย์ฉีดผม
lipstick	lipsatick	ลิปสติก
make - up	khrue-ang saam ung	เครื่องสำอาง
nail scissors	gangrai tut lep	กรรไกรตัดเล็บ
perfume	naam hom	น้ำหอม
powder	paeng	แป้ง
razor, shaver	meet kon	มีดโกน
shaving creme	kreem kon nuat	ครีมโกนหนวด
soap	saboo	สบู่
tissue	gradaat tishoo	กระดาษทิชชู่
toothbrush	praeng see fun	แปรงสีฟัน
toothpaste	yaa see fun	ยาสีฟัน
washcloth, flannel	fong naam	ฟองน้ำ

'praeng fun' = *brush one's teeth* แปรงฟัน
'gon nuat' = *shave* โกนหนวด

'wee phom' = *comb one's hair* หวีผม
'tat phom' = *cut one's hair* ตัดผม
'sa phom' = *shampoo one's hair* สระผม
'yoom phom' = *dye one's hair* ย้อมผม

Colours

colour	see	สี
dark colours	see gae	สีแก่
light colours	see on	สีอ่อน
colours of the rainbow	see roong	สีรุ้ง

beige	kaakee	กากี
black	dum	ดำ
brown	naamtaan	น้ำตาล
dark blue	naam ngoen	น้ำเงิน
dark brown	naamtaan kem	น้ำตาลเข้ม
dark green	khiao gae	เขียวแก่
gold	thong	ทอง
grey	thao	เทา
light blue	faa	ฟ้า
light green	khiao oon	เขียวอ่อน
orange	som	ส้ม
pink	chompoo	ชมพู
red	daeng	แดง
silver	ngoen	เงิน
violet	muang	ม่วง
white	khaao	ขาว
yellow	lue-ang	เหลือง

In the shop:

comparative: adjective + ***kwaa*** กว่า
superlative: adjective + ***thee sut*** ที่สุด

example: ***big -- bigger -- biggest***
yai -- yai kwaa -- yai thee sut
หญ่ ใหญ่กว่า ใหญ่ที่สุด

I go shopping.

Phom/chan pai sue khong.
ผม/ฉันไปซื้อของ

How much is it ?

Raakhaa thaorai ?
ราคาเท่าไหร่

That's a little bit too expensive !

Phaeng pai nooi !
แพงไปหน่อย

That's too expensive !

Phaeng goen pai !
แพงเกินไป

Can you reduce the price ?

Lot (raakhaa) daai mai ?
ลด(ราคา)ได้ไหม

Do you have something cheaper ?

Thook kwaa nee mee mai ?
ถูกกว่านี้มีไหม

Do you have it in a different colour ?

Mee see uen eek mai ?
มีสีอื่นอีกไหม

Can I try it on ?

Khaw long sai daai mai ?
ขอรองใส่ได้ไหม

That's too big - too small / too long - too short / too wide - too tight.

Nee yai-lek / yaao-san / luam-kap goen pai.
นี่ใหญ่-เล็ก / ยาว-สั้น / หลวม-คับ เกินไป

Do you have a bigger size ?

Khun mee thee yai kwaa nee mai khrap/kha ?
คุณมีที่ใหญ่กว่านี้ไหมครับ/ค่ะ

LIVING

House and apartment

chaao baan = *rent a house* เช่าบ้าน
chaao hong = *rent a room* เช่าห้อง
khaa chaao = *the rent* ค่าเช่า

basement, cellar	hong tai din	ห้องใต้ดิน
bathroom	hong naam	ห้องน้ำ
bedroom	hong non	ห้องนอน
building	tueg, akaan	ตึก, อาคาร
carpet	prom	พรม
curtain	phaa maan	ผ้าม่าน
door	pratoo, rua	ประตู, รั้ว
elevator	lif	ลิฟ
entrance	thaang khao	ทางเข้า
exit	thaang ok	ทางออก
fence	rua	รั้ว
floor	puen	พื้น
furniture	khreu-ang togteng baan	เครื่องตกแต่งบ้าน
garden	suan	สวน
gate, door	pratoo, rua	ประตู, รั้ว
house	baan	บ้าน
kitchen	hong krua	ห้องครัว
library	hong samut	ห้องสมุด
living room	hong nang len	ห้องนั่งเล่น
stairs, ladder	bandai	บันได
storey, floor	chan	ชั้น
swimming pool	sa wai naam	สระว่ายน้ำ
wall	panaang	ผนัง
window	naa taang	หน้าต่าง

Living room

hong nang len = *living room* ห้องนั่งเล่น

ashtray	thee kia buree	ที่เขี่ยบุหรี่
bookshelf	chan wang nangsue	ชั้นวางหนังสือ
chair	gao-ee	เก้าอี้
flower vase	chaek gan pak tokmai	แจกันปักดอกไม้
radio	withayu	วิทยุ
sofa	sofa	โซฟา
table	to	โต๊ะ
telephone	thorasap	โทรศัพท์
television	thoratat	โทรทัศน์

Bedroom

hong non = *bedroom* ห้องนอน

bed	tiang non	เตียงนอน
blanket	phaa hom	ผ้าห่ม
coat hanger	mai kwaen sue-a	ไม้แขวนเสื้อ
drawer	lin chak	ลิ้นชัก
duvet cover	phaa phoo thee non	ผ้าปูที่นอน
lamp	kom fai	โคมไฟ
make-up table	too khrue-ang baeng	โต๊ะเครื่องแป้ง
mattress	thee non	ที่นอน
pillow	mon	หมอน
pillowcase	plok mon	ปลอกหมอน
wardrobe, closet	too sue-a phaa	ตู้เสื้อผ้า

Kitchen

hong krua = *kitchen* ห้องครัว

bottle opener	thee poet kuat	ที่เปิดขวด
coffeemaker	khrue-ang tom kafae	เครื่องต้มกาแฟ
cooking pot	moo	หม้อ
dishwasher	khrue-ang lang chaan	เครื่องล้างจาน
fridge	too yen	ตู้เย็น
frying pan	kra ta	กระทะ
garbage bin	taang khaya	ถังขยะ
kitchen cupboard	chan wang chaan	ชั้นวางจาน
microwave oven	microwave	ไมโครเวฟ
sink	ung lung chaan	อ่างล้างจาน
stove, oven	dao op	เตาอบ
stove (electric)	dao fai faa	เตาไฟฟ้า
stove (gas)	dao gas	เตาแก๊ส
thermos flask	kratig naam rawn	กระติกน้ำร้อน
toaster	khrue-ang ping kanompang	เครื่องปิ้งขนมปัง

khrue-ang = *(electrical) appliances* เครื่อง

Bathroom

hong naam = *bathroom* ห้องน้ำ

bathtub	ung ab naam	อ่างอาบน้ำ
mirror	kratchok	กระจก
scales	khrue-ang chang naam nak	เครื่องชั่งน้ำหนัก
toilet	chakrok	ชักโครก
washbasin	ung lung naa	อ่างล้างหน้า
water tap	kok naam	ก็อกน้ำ

Useful words

aircondition	air	แอร์
broom	maai kwaat	ไม้กวาด
candle	tee-an	เทียน
(to) clean	tham kwaam sa aad	ทำความสะอาด
a clean room	hong thee sa aad	ห้องที่สะอาด
dry clothes on the clothesline	taak phaa	ตากผ้า
dust	fun	ฝุ่น
fan	pat lom	พัดลม
hammer	kon	ค้อน
handy, mobile phone	thorasap mue tue	โทรศัพท์มือถือ
iron	taao reet	เตารีด
launder clothes	sak phaa	ซักผ้า
light bulb	duang fai	ดวงไฟ

matches	maai keet fai	ไม้ขีดไฟ
mosquito net	mung	มุ้ง
picture	roobpaap	รูปภาพ
vacuum cleaner	khrue-ang toot fun	เครื่องดูดฝุ่น
washing machine	khrue-ang sak phaa	เครื่องซักผ้า
wipe	chet	เช็ด
wipe the floor	kwaat puen	กวาดพื้น

WORKING

Occupation --- Job

What do you work ?

Khun tham ngaan arai khrap ?
คุณทำงานอะไรครับ

Where do you work ?

Khun tham ngaan theenai khrap ?
คุณทำงานที่ไหนครับ

*Words, which describe different professions or occupations are mostly formed with **'chaang'** and **'nak'**.*

What is your profession ?

Khun mee aacheep arai khrap ?
คุณมีอาชีพอะไรครับ

***'chaang'** is mostly used for skilled workmen.*

profession	aacheep	อาชีพ
hobby	ngaan adeeraeg	งานอดิเรก
employee	phanak ngaan	พนักงาน
worker	khon ngaan	คนงาน

actor	nak sadaeng	นักแสดง
architect	satapanik	สถาปานิก
author, writer	nak khian	นักเขียน
boxer	nak muaai	นักมวย
cook (man)	pho khrua	พ่อครัว
cook (woman)	mae khrua	แม่ครัว
dancer	nak ten ram	นักเต้นรำ

dentist	mo fun	หมอฟัน
doctor	mo, paet	หมอ, แพทย์
electrician	chaang fai faa	ช่างไฟฟ้า
engineer	vitsavagon	วิศวกร
farmer	chaao naa	ชาวนา
fireman	panak ngaan tap ploeng	พนักงานดับเพลิง
fisherman	chaao pramong	ชาวประมง
gardener	khon tham suan	คนทำสวน
hairdresser	chaang tham phom	ช่างทำผม
lawyer	tanaai kwaam	ทนายความ
maid	khon rup chai	คนรับใช้
mechanic	chaang gon	ช่างกล
model (female)	nang baeb	นางแบบ
model (male)	nai baeb	นายแบบ
musician	nak dontree	นักดนตรี
nurse	phayaabaan	พยาบาล
painter	chaang taa see	ช่างทาสี
photographer	chaang paap	ช่างภาพ
pilot	nak bin	นักบิน
policeman	tamruat	ตำรวจ
postman	phoo rut praisanee	บุรุษไปรษณีย์
secretary	lae kaa noo gaan	เลขานุการ
(shop) assistant	phanak ngaan khaai	พนักงานขาย
singer	nak rong	นักร้อง
soldier	thahaan	ทหาร
teacher	khroo, achaan	ครู, อาจารย์
tailor	chaang tat sue-a	ช่างตัดเสื้อ

Business

bank	tanakaan	ธนาคาร
businessman	nak thurakit	นักธุรกิจ
company	borisat	บริษัท
diplomat	nak kaan thoot	นักการทูต
factory	rong ngaan	โรงงาน
farm	thoong naa	ทุ่งนา
grocery store	raan khaai khong cham	ร้านขายของชำ
industry	utsaha kam	อุตสาหกรรม
laundry	raan sak reet	ร้านซักรีด
manager	phoo chat gaan	ผู้จัดการ
owner	chao khong	เจ้าของ
pharmacy, drugstore	raan khaai yaa	ร้านขายยา
shop	raan	ร้าน

School

kindergarten, nursery	rong rian anoobaan	โรงเรียนอนุบาล
school	rong rian	โรงเรียน
primary school	prathom sueksaa	ประถมศึกษา
secondary school	mathayom sueksaa	มัธยมศึกษา
college, academy	vithayaalai	วิทยาลัย
university	mahaavithayaalai	มหาวิทยาลัย

absent	kat rian	ขาดเรียน
classroom	hong rian	ห้องเรียน
children's playground	sa naam dek len	สนามเด็กเล่น
homework	gaanbaan	การบ้าน
lesson	bot rian	บทเรียน
student, pupil	nak rian	นักเรียน
exam, test	sop	สอบ
fail the exam	sop tok	สอบตก
pass the exam	sop paan	สอบผ่าน
prepare for the exam	triam tua sop	เตรียมตัวสอบ
finish school	loek rian	เลิกเรียน

Do you play golf ?

Information to all golf resorts in Thailand !

Where to play & stay !

FAMILY

Family

family	khrop khrua	ครอบครัว
parents	pho mae	พ่อ, แม่
father	pho	พ่อ
mother	mae	แม่
wife	phanrayaa	ภรรยา
husband	saamee	สามี
son	look chaai	ลูกชาย
daugther	look saao	ลูกสาว
grandchild	laan	หลาน
younger brother	**nong** chaai	น้องชาย
elder brother	**phee** chaai	พี่ชาย
younger sister	nong saao	น้องสาว
elder sister	phee saao	พี่สาว
siblings	phee nong	พี่, น้อง

You have to distinguish between younger and elder persons.

'nong' *(younger person)* น้อง

'phee' *(elder person)* พี่

Relatives

You have to distinguish between relatives from your father or mother.

relatives	yaad	ญาติ
grandfather (of father)	poo	ปู่
grandfather (of mother)	taa	ตา
grandmother (of father)	yaa	ย่า
grandmother (of mother)	yaai	ยาย
uncle (= younger brother from father)	aa	อา
uncle (= younger brother from mother)	naa	น้า
uncle (= elder brother from father)	lung	ลุง
uncle (= elder brother from mother)	lung	ลุง
aunt (= younger sister from father)	aa	อา
aunt (= younger sister from mother)	naa	น้า
aunt (= elder sister from father)	paa	ป้า
aunt (= elder sister from mother)	paa	ป้า
niece	laan saao	หลานสาว
nephew	laan chaai	หลานชาย
cousin	look phee look nong	ลูกพี่ลูกน้อง
father-in-law	pho taa	พ่อตา
mother-in-law	mae yaai	แม่ยาย
son-in-law	look khoi	ลูกเขย
daughter-in-law	look saphai	ลูกสะใภ้

brother-in-law (husband of the elder sister)	phee khoi	พี่เขย
brother-in-law (husband of the younger sister)	nong khoi	น้องเขย
sister-in-law (wife of the elder brother)	phee saphai	พี่สะใภ้
sister-in-law (wife of the younger brother)	nong saphai	น้องสะใภ้

Useful words

baby, infant	taarok	ทารก
child	dek	เด็ก
teenager (generally)	wairun	วัยรุ่น
teenager (girl)	saao	สาว
teenager (boy)	num	หนุ่ม
adult, grown-up	phoo yai	ผู้ใหญ่
friend	phue-an	เพื่อน
girlfriend / boyfriend	faen	แฟน
single	sot	โสด
married	taengnaan	แต่งงาน
widowed	maai	ม้าย
divorced	yaa	หย่า
wife (colloquial)	mia luang	เมียหลวง
mistress	mia noi	เมียน้อย

DOCTOR's OFFICE

mo = *doctor* หมอ
mo fun = *dentist* หมอฟัน
phayaabaan = *nurse* พยาบาล
rong phayaabaan = *hospital* โรงพยาบาล

You should see a doctor.

Khit waa khun khuan pai haa mo.
คิดว่าคุณควรไปหาหมอ

Help ! = ***chuai duai !*** ช่วยด้วย

I don't feel very well.

Roosuek mai sabaai. Phom mai sabaai.
รู้สึกไม่สบาย, ผมไม่สบาย

I am feeling (getting) sick.

Roosuek yaak adshee-an.
รู้สึกอยากอาเจียน

I feel dizzy.

Roosuek wee-an hua.
รู้สึกเวียนหัว

I feel very weak (faintness).

Roosuek cha pen lom.
รู้สึกจะเป็นลม

Where does it hurt ?

Chaep thee nai ?
เจ็บที่ไหน

It hurts here.

Chaep trong nee.
เจ็บตรงนี้

Take three pills (twice) daily.

Kin yaa saam met wun la khrung (soong khrung).
กินยาสามเม็ดวันละครั้ง(สองครั้ง)

Body

body	raang gaai, tua	ร่างกาย, ตัว
ankle	ko thaao	ข้อเท้า
arm	khaen	แขน
back	lung	หลัง
beard	krao	เครา
blood	lueat	เลือด
bone	gratook	กระดูก
bottom, buttocks	gon	ก้น
brain	samong	สมอง
breast	nom	นม
cheek	gaem	แก้ม
chest, breast	na ok	หน้าอก
chin	kaang	คาง
ear	hoo	หู
elbow	koo soog	ข้อศอก
eye	taa	ตา
eyebrow	kiw	คิ้ว
face	naa	หน้า

finger	niw	นิ้ว
fingernail	lep mue	เล็บมือ
foot	thaao	เท้า
forehead	naa paak	หน้าผาก
genitals	awaiyawa phaet	อวัยวะเพศ
hair	phom	ผม
hand	mue	มือ
head	hua	หัว
heart	hua jai	หัวใจ
hip	sa poog	สะโพก
knee	hua kao	หัวเข่า
leg	khaa	ขา
lip	rim fee paak	ริมฝีปาก
liver	tap	ตับ
lung	pood	ปอด
mouth	paak	ปาก
muscle	glaam, glaam nuea	กล้าม, กล้ามเนื้อ
mustache	nuat	หนวด
neck	lum kho	ลำคอ
nerve	sen prasaat	เส้นประสาท
nose	chamook	จมูก
shoulder	ba, lai, ba lai	บ่า,ไหล่, บ่าไหล่
skin	phiw, phiw nang	ผิว, ผิวหนัง
sole	fa thaao	ฝ่าเท้า
stomach	thawng	ท้อง
sweat	nguea	เหงื่อ
toenail	lep thaao	เล็บเท้า

tongue	lin	ลิ้น
tooth	fun	ฟัน
waist	eu	เอว
wrist	koo mue	ข้อมือ

Health and Illness

airsick	mao khrueang bin	เมาเครื่องบิน
allergy	poom pae	ภูมิแพ้
asthma	rok huet	โรคหืด
backache	puat lung	ปวดหลัง
bleed	lueat ok	เลือดออก
bruise	rabom, cham	ระบม, ช้ำ
burn	mee plae maai	มีแผลไหม้
cancer	maraeng	มะเร็ง
caries, tooth decay	fun phoo	ฟันผุ
carsick	mao rot	เมารถ
cholera	ahiwaa	อหิวา
cold	pen vat	เป็นหวัด
cough	ai	ไอ
cramp	ta khriw	ตะคริว
death	kwaam taai	ความตาย
diabetes	rok baao waan	โรคเบาหวาน
diarrhoea	thawng sia	ท้องเสีย
disease, illness	pen rok	เป็นโรค
faint, unconscious	pen lom	เป็นลม
fever	mee khai	มีไข้

flu, influenza	khai vat yai	ไข้หวัดใหญ่
fracture	hag	หัก
hangover	mao kaang	เมาค้าง
headache	puat hua	ปวดหัว
(good) health	sukhaphaap (dee)	สุขภาพ(ดี)
hurt, pain	chaep, puat	เจ็บ, ปวด
hurt, pain(momentary)	chaep	เจ็บ
hurt, pain (permanent)	puat	ปวด
ideal weight	naam nak maat da taan	น้ำหนักมาตราฐาน
ill, sick	puai, mai sabaai	ป่วย, ไม่สบาย
infection	tit chuea	ติดเชื้อ
insect bite	don malaeng cut	โดนแมลงกัด
injury	baat chaep	บาดเจ็บ
life	cheewit	ชีวิต
malaria	malaria	มาลาเรีย
pain	puat	ปวด
pneumonia	rok pod ak saep	โรคปอดอักเสบ
pregnant	dang kan, mee thawng	ตั้งครรภ์, มีท้อง
seasick	mao ruea	เมาเรือ
sore throat	chaep kho	เจ็บคอ
sprain	khlaet	เคล็ด
stomach-ache	puat thawng	ปวดท้อง
sunburn	taet paao	แดดเผา
toothache	puat fun	ปวดฟัน
venereal disease	gama rok	กามโรค
vomit	adcheean	อาเจียน
wound	baat plae	บาดแผล

Medical Treatment

aspirin	aspirin	แอสไพริน
bandage	phaa pan pae	ผ้าพันแผล
diat	lot ahaan	ลดอาหาร
examine	truat	ตรวจ
exercise	ok gum lung gaai	ออกกำลังกาย
health	sukhaphaap	สุขภาพ
injection	cheet yaa	ฉีดยา
insulin	yaa gae rok baao waan	ยาแก้โรคเบาหวาน
medical treatment	ruksaa, doo lae	รักษา, ดูแล
medicine	yaa	ยา
morphine	morfin	มอร์ฟีน
painkiller	yaa gae puat	ยาแก้ปวด
pill, tablet	yaa met	ยาเม็ด
plaster	phalastaa	พลาสเตอร์
prescription	bai sung yaa	ใบสั่งยา
sleeping pill	yaa non lap	ยานอนหลับ

Are you in a hurry?

All you need to keep going.

This little book will help you get by in Thailand!

Now in it's 3rd revised and updated edition !

POST OFFICE & BANK

Important words

account	banchee	บัญชี
airmail	praisanee aakaat	ไปรษณีย์อากาศ
bank	tanaakaan	ธนาคาร
check	check	เช็ค
envelope	song chotmaai	ซองจดหมาย
express	duan	ด่วน
interest	dok bee-a	ดอกเบี้ย
letter	chotmaai	จดหมาย
letterbox, mailbox	too praisanee	ตู้ไปรษณีย์
money	ngoen	เงิน
newspaper	nangsue pim	หนังสือพิมพ์
packet	patsadoo	พัสดุ
parcel, box	ho, ho khong	ห่อ, ห่อของ
postman	phoo rut praisanee	บุรุษไปรษณีย์
stamp	sa taem, praisanee yagon	แสตมป์, ไปรษณียากร
postcard	praisanee yabat	ไปรษณียบัตร
post office	praisanee	ไปรษณีย์
receipt	bai set	ใบเสร็จ
telegram	thoralaek	โทรเลข
traveler's check	check doenthaang	เช็คเดินทาง

receive a letter	rup chotmaai	รับจดหมาย
register a letter	long thabian	ลงทะเบียน
send a letter	song chotmaai	ส่งจดหมาย
type a letter	pim chotmaai	พิมพ์จดหมาย
borrow money	kho yuem ngoen	ขอยืมเงิน
change money	laek ngoen	แลกเงิน
deposit money	faak ngoen	ฝากเงิน
earn money	haa ngoen	หาเงิน
lend money	haai yuem ngoen	ให้ยืมเงิน
save money	kaep ngoen	เก็บเงิน
spend money	chaai ngoen	ใช้เงิน, เสียเงิน
waste money	sia daai ngoen	เสียดายเงิน
withdraw money	thon ngoen	ถอนเงิน
be in debt	pen nee	เป็นหนี้
economical	brayat ngoen	ประหยัดเงิน

Additional words

application	bai samak	ใบสมัคร
application (for a job)	gaan samak	การสมัคร
book	nangsue	หนังสือ
coin	reean	เหรียญ
deposit	matcham	มัดจำ
document	egasaan	เอกสาร
eraser, rubber	yaang lob	ยางลบ
glue, adhesive	gaao	กาว

ink	naam muek	น้ำหมึก
magazine, periodical	nit dta ya saan	นิตยสาร
map	paen tee	แผนที่
notebook	samut	สมุด
passport	nangsue doenthaang	หนังสือเดินทาง
pen	paakkaa	ปากกา
pencil	deenso	ดินสอ
ruler	maai ban tat	ไม้บรรทัด
writing paper	gradaat	กระดาษ

Examples : Post Office & Bank

Where is the nearest post office ?

Praisanee thee glai theesoot yuu theenai khrap/kha ?
ไปรษณีย์ที่ใกล้ที่สุดอยู่ที่ไหนครับ/ค่ะ

What time is the bank open ?

Tanaakaan poet kee mawng khrap/kha ?
ธนาคารเปิดกี่โมงครับ/ค่ะ

Can I change traveler's checks here?

Khuen check doenthaang thee nee daai mai ?
ขึ้นเช็คเดินทางที่นี่ได้ไหม

Can I see your passport ?

Khaw doo nangsue doenthaang nooi daai mai ?
ขอดูหนังสือเดินทางหน่อยได้ไหม

This passport is expired.

Nangsue doenthaang mot aayoo laew.
หนังสือเดินทางหมดอายุแล้ว

Can you give me some small change?

Laek ngoen nooi daai mai ?
แลกเงินหน่อยได้ไหม

Please change to ....

Khaw laek ngoen pen ngoen.....
ขอแลกเงินเป็นเงิน....

Can I change these traveler's checks ?

Khaw laek chek doenthaang daai mai ?
ขอแลกเช็คเดินทางได้ไหม

Could you count the coins ?

Khun chuai nap reean daai mai khrap ?
คุณช่วยนับเหรียญได้ไหมครับ

How long does mail take to Europe?

Song chotmaai pai europe chaai waelaa thaorai ?
ส่งจดหมายไปยุโรปใช้เวลาเท่าไหร่

How much is a letter to Europe?

Song chotmaai pai europe raakaa thaorai ?
ส่งจดหมายไปยุโรปราคาเท่าไหร่

TELEPHONE

Useful words

tho = *to phone* โทร
tho pai = *phone somebody* โทรไป
tho maa = *phone from somewhere* โทรมา
tho glup = *phone back* โทรกลับ
to saai = *connect* ต่อสาย

mobile phone, handy	thorasap mue tue	โทรศัพท์มือถือ
telephone	thorasap	โทรศัพท์
telephone bill	khaa thorasap	ค่าโทรศัพท์
telephone book	samut thorasap	สมุดโทรศัพท์
telephone box	too thorasap	ตู้โทรศัพท์
telephone number	boe thorasap	เบอร์โทรศัพท์
answer the phone	rup thorasap	รับโทรศัพท์
phone somebody	thorasap, tho	โทรศัพท์,โทร

overseas call	thorasap thaang prathaet โทรศัพท์ต่างประเทศ
collect call	thorasap kep ngoen plai thaang โทรศัพท์เก็บเงินปลายทาง
operator	panak ngaan rup thorasap พนักงานรับโทรศัพท์

Examples: On the phone

Can I make an overseas call from here ?

Cha thorasap pai thaang prathaet chaak theenee daai mai ?
จะโทรศัพท์ไปต่างประเทศจากที่นี่ได้ไหม

How much is the phone call to Europe ?

Thorasap pai europe thaorai ?
โทรศัพท์ไปยุโรปเท่าไหร่

Do you have a telephone listing ?

Mee samut thorasap mai ?
มีสมุดโทรศัพท์ไหม

I would like to make a collect call.

Kep ngoen plai thaang.
เก็บเงินปลายทาง

Hello,...............speaking

Hello,....phoot.
ฮัลโหล,....พูด

With whom would you like to speak ?

Toong gaan phoot gap khrai khrap ?
ต้องการพูดกลับใครครับ

Who is speaking ?

Khrai phoot khrap ?
ใครพูดครับ

Could I speak with Ms Wasana, please ?

Khaw phoot gap Khun Wasana noi khrap/ka ?
ขอพูดกับคุณวาสนาหน่อยครับ/ค่ะ

I speak with Ms Wasana, don't I ?

Khun Wasana phoot chai mai ?
คุณวาสนาพูดใช่ไหม

Yes, it's me.

Gamlang phoot yuu kha.
กำลังพูดอยู่ค่ะ

She is not here !

Khao mai yuu !
เขาไม่อยู่

Do you know where she is?

Khun saap mai waa khao yuu theenai ?
คุณทราบไหมว่าเขาอยู่ที่ไหน

Can I leave a message for Lek ?

Khaw faak kho kwaam thueng Khun Lek daai mai ?
ขอฝากข้อความถึงคุณเล็กได้ไหม

Would you like to leave a message ?

Mee arai cha sang mai ?
มีอะไรจะสั่งไหม

Please tell her that Mr. Peter called.

Garunaa bawk khao duai waa Khun Peter tho maa.
กรุณาบอกเขาด้วยว่าคุณปีเตอร์โทรมา

Please leave following message:

Garunaa faak kho khwaam duai na khrap/kha:
กรุนาฝากข้อความด้วยนะครับ/ค่ะ

I will tell her that you called.

Cha bawk khao waa khun tho maa.
จะบอกเขาว่าคุณโทรมา

Please tell her that she should call me back.

Garunaa bawk khao haai tho glup duai.
กรุณาบอกเขาให้โทรกลับด้วย

I will call again later.

Diaw cha tho maa mai / Cha tho maa eek.
เดี๋ยวจะโทรมาใหม่ / จะโทรมาอีก

Please call again tomorrow.

Garunaa tho maa mai phrung nee.
กรุณาโทรมาใหม่พรุ่งนี้

Please speak more slowly !

Chuai phoot chaa chaa nooi !
ช่วยพูดช้าๆหน่อย

Please speak louder !

Chuai phoot dung dung nooi !
ช่วยพูดดังๆหน่อย

Please say again !

Chuai phoot eek khrung !
ช่วยพูดอีกครั้ง

I don't understand.

Phom mai khao jai.
ผมไม่เข้าใจ

Pardon me ? I didn't get that.

Phom fang mai tan.
ผมฟังไม่ทัน

I dialed a wrong number.

Phom tho pit.
ผมโทรผิด

I will call again tomorrow at around 6 o'clock in the morning.

Cha tho maa mai phrung nee pramaan hok mawng chaao.
จะโทรมาใหม่พรุ่งนี้ประมาณ ๖ โมงเช้า

Please be home.

Garunaa yuu baan.
กรุณาอยู่บ้าน

My regards to Lek.

Bawk sawatdee Lek duai.
บอกสวัสดีเล็กด้วย

The line is busy.

Saai mai waang.
สายไม่ว่าง

Nobody answers.

Mai mee khrai rup saai.
ไม่มีใครรับสาย

One moment, please.

Ro suk khroo khrap/kha. Khooi diaw khrap/kha.
รอสักครู่ครับ/ค่ะ. คอยเดี๋ยวครับ/ค่ะ

That would be everything.

Khae nee na khrap/kha.
แค่นี้นะครับ/ค่ะ

English - Thai - All you have to know

Available as pocket book

P a p e r b a c k

NATURE

Animals and Insects

animal	sat	สัตว์
zoo	suan sat	สวนสัตว์
ant	mot	มด
bat	khaang khaao	ค้างคาว
bear	mee	หมี
bee	pueng	ผึ้ง
beetle	malaeng	แมลง
bird	nok	นก
butterfly	phee sue-a	ผีเสื้อ
calf	look vua	ลูกวัว
camel	oot	อูฐ
cat	maew (tua mia)	แมว(ตัวเมีย)
(tom) cat	maew tua phoo	แมวตัวผู้
cattle	vua	วัว
chicken	gai	ไก่
cobra	ngoo hao	งูเห่า
cockroach	malaeng saap	แมลงสาบ
cow	vua	วัว
crocodile	chorakhae	จระเข้
dog	maa	หมา
duck	pet	เป็ด
elephant	chaang	ช้าง
fish	plaa	ปลา
fly	malaeng wun	แมลงวัน

frog	gop	กบ
game	gwaang	กวาง
gecko	took kae	ตุ๊กแก
giraffe	jeeraf	ยีราฟ
goat	pae	แพะ
horse	maa	ม้า
insect	malaeng	แมลง
kangaroo	chingchaw	จิงโจ้
leopard	sue-a taw	เสือดาว
lion	sing to	สิงโต
lizard	ching chok	จิ้งจก
monkey	ling	ลิง
mosquito	yung	ยุง
mouse, rat	noo	หนู
owl	nok hook	นกฮูก
parrot	nok gaeaw	นกแก้ว
pig	moo	หมู
rabbit	grataai	กระต่าย
scorpion	maeng pong	แมงป่อง
shark	plaa chalaam	ปลาฉลาม
snake	ngoo	งู
spider	maeng mum	แมงมุม
squid	plaa muek	ปลาหมึก
tiger	sue-a	เสือ
turtle	tao	เต่า
whale	plaa waan	ปลาวาฬ
wild boar	moo paa	หมูป่า

Landscape

'lom' = *wind* ลม
'lom on on' = *breeze* ลมอ่อนๆ
'lom chooi' = *breeze* ลมโชย
'lom phut' = *windy* ลมพัด
'lom phut raeng' = *very windy* ลมพัดแรง

air	aagaat	อากาศ
bay	aw	อ่าว
beach	chai haat	ชายหาด
cape	laem	แหลม
cave	tham	ถ้ำ
channel, canal	klong	คลอง
cloud	maek	เมฆ
coast	fang thalae, chai thalae	ฝั่งทะเล, ชายทะเล
coral	hin pagaarang	หินปะการัง
dam	khuean	เขื่อน
desert	thalae saai	ทะเลทราย
earth	din	ดิน
earthquake	phaen din wai	แผ่นดินไหว
field	rai naa, puen naa	ไร่นา, ผืนนา
fire	fai	ไฟ
fog	mok	หมอก
heat	kwaam rawn	ความร้อน
island	kho	เกาะ
jungle	baa tuep	ป่าทึบ
lake	thalae saap	ทะเลสาป
lightning	faa paa	ฟ้าผ่า

'naam long' = *low tide* น้ำลง
'naam khuen' = *high tide* น้ำขึ้น
'naam thuam' = *flood* น้ำท่วม

moon	duang chan, pra chan	ดวงจันทร์, พระจันทร์
moor, swamp	bueng, nong	บึง, หนอง
mountain	phookhao	ภูเขา
nature	thamma chaat	ธรรมชาติ
park	suan	สวน
reef, rock	naa phaa	หน้าผา
rice field	naa kaao	นาข้าว
river	mae naam	แม่น้ำ
sand	saai	ทราย
sea	thalae	ทะเล
sky	faa	ฟ้า
snow	hima	หิมะ
star	daaw	ดาว
stone	hin	หิน
sun	duang aathit, pra aathit	ดวงอาทิตย์, พระอาทิตย์
thunder	faa rawng	ฟ้าร้อง
waterfall	naam tok	น้ำตก
weather	aagaat	อากาศ
wood, forest	baa	ป่า

' pra aathit khuen' = *sunrise* พระอาทิตย์ขึ้น
' pra aathit tok' = *sunset* พระอาทิตย์ตก

Different plants

'tok maai' = *flower* ดอกไม้
'ton maai' = *tree* ต้นไม้

bamboo	ton phai	ต้นไผ่
brushes, shrubbery	poom maai	พุ่มไม้
grass	yaa	หญ้า
jasmine	tok malee	ดอกมะลิ
lotus	tok bua	ดอกบัว
orchid	kluai maai	กล้วยไม้
palm tree	ton plaam	ต้นปาล์ม
plant	phuet	พืช
rose	kulaab	กุหลาบ
teak tree	ton sak	ต้นสัก
wood	maai	ไม้

TRAVEL

Useful travel words

aircondition	khrueang aer	เครื่องแอร์
airline	saai gaan bin	สายการบิน
airplane	khrueang bin	เครื่องบิน
airport	sanaam bin	สนามบิน
arrival	thueng	ถึง
bicycle	rot chakrayaan	รถจักรยาน
bus (regular)	rot thammadaa	รถธรรมดา
bus (with aircondition)	rot prap agaat	รถปรับอากาศ
bus station	satanee rot bus	สถานีรถบัส
bus stop	paai rot mae	ป้ายรถเมล์
car	rot	รถ
crash helmet	muak gun nok	หมวกกันน็อค
departure	ok	ออก
document	aegasaan	เอกสาร
ferry	ruea kaam faak	เรือข้ามฟาก
hotel	rong raem	โรงแรม
motorbike	rot chakrayaan yon	รถจักรยานยนต์
railway	rot fai	รถไฟ
railway station	satanee rot fai	สถานีรถไฟ
room with aircondition	hong aer	ห้องแอร์
seaport, harbour	thaa ruea	ท่าเรือ
ship	ruea	เรือ
sight-seeing	borigaan gaan tong thiaw	บริการการท่องเที่ยว

Examples: Traveling

hong koo *= room with twin beds* ห้องคู่
hong diaw *= room with double bed* ห้องเดี่ยว

Do you have rooms vacant ?

Mee hong waang mai ?
มีห้องว่างไหม

How much is the night ?

Khaa hong wan la thaorai ?
ค่าห้องวันละเท่าไหร่

How long will you stay ?

Khun cha yuu naan thaorai ?
คุณจะอยู่นานเท่าไหร่

I don't know yet how long.

Mai saap waa cha yuu naan thaorai.
ไม่ทราบว่าจะอยู่นานเท่าไหร่

Can I see the room ?

Khaw doo hong gon daai mai ?
ขอดูห้องก่อนได้ไหม

Could you bring my luggage, please?

Chuai yok grapao maa haai nooi daai mai ?
ช่วยยกกระเป๋ามาให้หน่อยได้ไหม

Can I put something into the safe ?

Khaw faak khong wai nai too saef daai mai ?
ขอฝากของไว้ในตู้เซฟได้ไหม

Can I order food to the room ?

Sang ahaan maa thaan bon hong daai mai ?
สั่งอาหามารทานบนห้องได้ไหม

Could you please give me a wake-up call at 6:00 AM ?

Chuai plook phom waelaa 6 mawng chaao daai mai ?
ช่วยปลุกผมเวลา ๖ โมงเช้าได้ไหม

My room number is...

Phom yuu hong boe ...
ผมอยู่ห้องเบอร์...

I will depart tomorrow.

Phom cha pai phrung nee.
ผมจะไปพรุ่งนี้

khuen = *get on* ขึ้น
long = *get off* ลง
Be careful however:
long ruea = *get on the boat* ลงเรือ
khuen chaak ruea = *get off the boat* ขึ้นจากเรือ

Traveling by train

express train	rot duan	รถด่วน
fast train	rot rae-o	รถเร็ว
first class	chan nueng	ชั้นหนึ่ง
left-luggage office	thee faak grapao	ที่ฝากกระเป๋า
platform	chaan cha laa	ชานชลา
railway	rot fai	รถไฟ
railway station	satanee rot fai	สถานีรถไฟ
reservation	chong tua	จองตั๋ว
return ticket	tua pai glup	ตั๋วไปกลับ
sleeping car	rot non	รถนอน
ticket	tua	ตั๋ว
ticket office	chong khaai tua	ช่องขายตั๋ว
timetable	taa raang rot fai	ตารางรถไฟ

What time is the train to Chiang Mai leaving ?

Rot fai pai Chiang Mai ok kee mawng ?
รถไฟไปเชียงใหม่ออกกี่โมง

Train to Chiang Mai leaves at 15:00 from platform 1.

Rot fai pai Chiang Mai cha ok chaan cha laa thee 1 waelaa baai 3 mawng.
รถไฟไปเชียงใหม่จะออกชานชลาที่ ๑ เวลาบ่าย ๓ โมง

Tickets, please !

Kho doo tua nooi khrap !
ขอดูตั๋วหน่อยครับ

Traveling by car

tem tung = *fill up* เต็มถัง
khrueng tung = *half full* ครึ่งถัง

accident	ubadtee haed	อุบัติเหตุ
break down	sia	เสีย
car	rot	รถ
car park	thee chot rot	ที่จอดรถ
car rental charge	khaa chaao rot	ค่าเช่ารถ
detour	thaang om	ทางอ้อม
drive	wing	วิ่ง
drive, steer	khup	ขับ
driving licence	pai khup kee	ใบขับขี่
garage	rong kep rot	โรงเก็บรถ
insurance	pragan	ประกัน
intersection, junction	see yaek	สี่แยก
limousine service	borigan rot rup song	บริการรถรับส่ง
park	chot rot	จอดรถ
petrol station	pam naam man	ปั๊มน้ำมัน
refuel	toem naam man	เติมน้ำมัน
(in) reverse gear, back into	tooi lung, tooi rot	ถอยหลัง, ถอยรถ
short cut	thaang lat	ทางลัด
stop	chot rot	จอดรถ
take a ride	nang rot len	นั่งรถเล่น
take over	saeng	แซง
tax	paasee	ภาษี
tow off	laak rot	ลากรถ

traffic	cha raa chon	จราจร
traffic jam	rot tit	รถติด
traffic lights	fai cha raa chon	ไฟจราจร
turn	liaw	เลี้ยว
turn around, U-turn	glup rot	กลับรถ

Mechanics

automatic transmission	automatik, atanomat	ออโตเมติก, อัตโมมัต
boot, trunk	grabprong lung rot	กระโปรงหลังรถ
brake	braek	เบรค
clutch	klut	ครัช
engine	khrueang yon	เครื่องยนต์
exhaust	to ai sia	ท่อไอเสีย
gear, gear shift	gee-a	เกียร์
headlight	fai naa rot	ไฟหน้ารถ
indicator	fai liaw	ไฟเลี้ยว
petrol, gasoline	naam man	น้ำมัน
rear light, taillight	fai tai rot	ไฟท้ายรถ
rearview mirror, mirror	gratchok	กระจก
repair	som rot	ซ่อมรถ
speedometer	khrueang wat kwaam rae-o	เครื่องวัดความเร็ว
steering wheel	puang ma lai	พวงมาลัย
tyre	yung rot	ยางรถ
used car	rot chaai laew	รถใช้แล้ว
V-belt	sai paan	สายพาน
wheel	lo rot	ล้อรถ
windscreen, windshield	gratchok naa rot	กระจกหน้ารถ
windscreen wiper	thee pat naam fon	ที่ปัดน้ำฝน

rot staat mai tit = *the engine won't start* รถสตาร์ทไม่ติด
rot sia = *the car is broken* รถเสีย

Please check the tyre pressure !

Check lom yung haai duai !
เช็คลมยางให้ด้วย

Can you repair the car here ?

Theenee som rot daai mai ?
ที่นี่ซ่อมรถได้ไหม

There is something wrong with the brakes.

Braek mai kooi dee.
เบรคไม่ค่อยดี

How long will it take to repair the car ?

Chaai waelaa som naan praman thaorai ?
ใช้เวลาซ่อมนานประมาณเท่าไหร่

Where can I park the car ?

Chot daai theenai ?
จอดได้ที่ไหน

yung taek = *tyre blowout* ยางแตก
yung faeb = *puncture, flat tyre* ยางแฟบ

I would like to rent a car.

Phom tongaan chaao rot.
ผมต้องการเช่ารถ

On the road

No turn !	haam liaw	ห้ามเลี้ยว
Danger ! Caution !	rawang	ระวัง
No entry !	haam kao	ห้ามเข้า
No traffic allowed !	haam rot took chanit wing	ห้ามรถทุกชนิดวิ่ง
No horn !	haam chaai see-ang	ห้ามใช้เสียง
Keep left !	chit saai	ชิดซ้าย
No parking !	haam chot	ห้ามจอด
Sharp bend ahead !	kong antaraai	โค้งอันตราย
No overtaking !	haam saeng	ห้ามแซง
No U-turn !	haam glup rot	ห้ามกลับรถ

City and Country

tit nuea = *north* ทิศเหนือ
tit tai = *south* ทิศใต้
tit tawan tok = *west* ทิศตะวันตก
tit tawan ok = *east* ทิศตะวันออก

abroad	taang prathaet	ต่างประเทศ
address	thee yuu	ที่อยู่
capital city	mueang luang	เมืองหลวง
city, town	mueang	เมือง
country	prathaet	ประเทศ
district	ampoe	อำเภอ
lane	sooi	ซอย
precinct	tambon	ตำบล

province	changwat	จังหวัด
street	thanon	ถนน
village	moo baan	หมู่บ้าน
world	lok	โลก
Europe	yurop	ยุโรป
Thailand	thai	ไทย
Australia	awsatralia	ออสเตรเลีย
England	ungkrit	อังกฤษ
USA	saharat america	สหรัฐอเมริกา
Cambodia	khamaen	เขมร
Laos	laao	ลาว
Malaysia	maalaesia	มาเลเซีย
Myanmar	phamaa	พม่า

Directions

saai = *left* ซ้าย
khwaa = *right* ขวา
trong pai = *straight ahead* ตรงไป

above	khaang bon	ข้างบน
around	rob	รอบ
around the world	rob lok	รอบโลก
behind	daan laang	ด้านหลัง
corner	mum	มุม
here	thee nee	ที่นี่
in front	daan naa	ด้านหน้า
in the middle of	trong glaang	ตรงกลาง
in, at	nai	ใน
inside	khaang nai	ข้างใน
next to, beside	daan khaang	ด้านข้าง
opposite	trong khaam	ตรงข้าม
on the left	khaang saai	ข้างซ้าย
on the right	khaang khwaa	ข้างขวา
outside	khaang nok	ข้างนอก
over there	thee noon	ที่โน่น
there	thee nan	ที่นั่น
under	khaang laang	ข้างล่าง
up to, as far as	chon thueng	จนถึง

More examples

Is this the way to Pattaya ?

Nee thanon pai Pattaya chai mai ?
นี่ถนนไปพัทยาใช่ไหม

Which way to Pattaya ?

Pai Pattaya pai thaang nai ?
ไปพัทยาไปทางไหน

How long does it take to Pattaya ?

Pai Pattaya chaai waelaa naan thaorai ?
ไปพัทยาใช้เวลานานเท่าไหร่

What time does the first (last) bus leave for Chonburi ?

Rot thiaw raek (sut taai) pai Chonburi kee mạwng ?
รถเที่ยวแรก(สุดท้าย)ไปชลบุรีกี่โมง

What a traffic jam today !

Wun nee rot tit maak chai mai ?
วันนี้รถติดมากใช่ไหม

Is it always like this ?

Pen yung nee took wun rue plaao ?
เป็นยังงี้ทุกวันหรือเปล่า

You can bet on it. There is always traffic like this.

Nae non. Rot tit yung nee took wun.
แน่นอน. รถติดอย่างนี้ทุกวัน

I better walk.

Phom khit waa phom doen dee kwaa.
ผมคิดว่าผมเดินดีกว่า

It is too far to walk.

Thaang glai maak.
ทางไกลมาก

Pleasant journey !

Thiaw haai sanuk na khrap !
เที่ยวให้สนุกนะครับ

Do you play golf ?

Golf Resorts of Thailand

Where to play & stay

www.golfasian.com

Up-to-date information on all golf resorts in Thailand !

FEELINGS

'Heart' - words

Many words which describe feelings begin or end with the word **'jai'**, which actually means **heart**.

Following some important '**heart**' words with short explanations.

aw jai เอาใจ **to take care of someone**

*If you take care about somebody, then you are **'aw jai'** to this person.*

aw jai tua aeng เอาใจตัวเอง **selfish**

*If you don't care about others and only think about you, then you will hear **'aw jai tua eng'**.*

chaèp jai เจ็บใจ **hurt (emotionally)**

*Your wife finds out that you have a minor wife. Your wife will feel **'chaèp jai'**. Be careful.*

ching jai จริงใจ **honest**

You are honest to others and say the truth. You don't hide your feelings

*You have a'honest heart', you are **'ching jai'**.*

chuea jai เชื่อใจ **trust, believe**

You believe in somebody, trust someone, you believe in the 'heart' of the other person.

chuen jai ชื่นใจ **pleased**

You are happy, pleased about something or somebody.

*You are **'chuen jai'**.*

dee jai ดีใจ **glad**
You can come back to Thailand after a long time and you will be feeling ***'dee jai'****. This is used frequently for different occassions, but do not confuse it with* ***'jai dee'****.*

glum jai กลุ้มใจ **concerned, worried**
Your daughter neglects her education and only enjoys her free time. You feel ***'glum jai'****.*

hua jai หัวใจ **heart**
This means heart.

hua jai wai หัวใจวาย **heart attack**
Used as verb, it means heart attack.
Used as noun, it means somebody had a heart attack and died.

jai boon, jai on ใจบุญ, ใจอ่อน **kind, ready to help**
You help others who need help. You give money for charity. You are ***'jai boon'*** *or* ***'jai on'****.*

jai daet ใจเด็ด **resolute, brave**
You take risks and have every situation under control.
You are ***'jai daet'****.*

jai dam ใจดำ **careless, ruthless**
Your friend needs your help, but you do not care.
They will say you are ***'jai dam'****.*

jai dee ใจดี **nice, pleasant**
You help somebody or you are doing somebody a favour without asking.
You will hear the compliment ***'jai dee'****.*

jai diaw ใจเดียว **faithful**

You are faithful to your partner. You are ***'jai diaw'****.*

jai mee lai hong ใจมีหลายห้อง **ladykiller, Casanova**

You have a few girlfriends at the same time. You are not serious with anybody. Your heart has 'many rooms' (=lai hong).

jai ngaai ใจง่าย **easily influenced**

You are a person who can be easily manipulated, you do what others say.
You have an easy heart, have ***'jai ngaai'****.*

jai nooi ใจน้อย **sensitive**

Your heart is hurt easily. You are emotionally hurt very often.

jai pam ใจป้ำ **generous**

You are going out with friends. When it's time to pay the bill,you pay everything.You are ***'jai pam'****.*

jai raai ใจร้าย **bad, evil, nasty**

A bad word. You are unscrupulous and don't care at all about others.

jai rawn ใจร้อน **angry, upset**

You get upset easily. You have a 'hot heart', you are ***'jai rawn'****. You will hear* ***'jai yen yen'****.*

jai ten ใจเต้น **nervous, excited**

You are excited, nervous about something. You feel ***'jai ten'****.*

jai yen ใจเย็น **calm, cool**
You are in a traffic jam on your way to the airport and miss your plane. However, you are not angry, you stay cool, have ***'jai yen'****. You will hear this word very often. Should you lose your temper, you will hear* ***'jai yen yen'****.*

khao jai เข้าใจ **understand**
You understand what is said or done.

kraeng jai เกรงใจ **considerate, kind**
You are sitting in a non-smoking taxi. You do not care about this and smoke. The taxi driver does not say anything and let you smoke.
He is ***'kraeng jai'****.*
This is one of the most important heart words.
Everybody will try to be ***'kraeng jai'****.*

lang lae jai ลังเลใจ **undecided, irresolute**
You cannot make a decision, you are thinking a long time how to decide, you are ***'lang lae jai'****.*

mun jai มั่นใจ **confident**
You are absolutely sure with your feelings to your girlfriend. You are ***'mun jai'****. You also will hear this in TV spots and advertisements.*

nae jai แน่ใจ **sure**
You are sure about something, similar to ***'mun jai'****.*

nak jai หนักใจ **concerned, worried**
Your children don't do what you think is good for them; you are worried, feel ***'nak jai'****.*

nok jai นอกใจ **cheat, deceive**
*You cheat, deceive on your partner, you are **'nok jai'**.*

phum jai ภูมิใจ **proud**
You are proud of something or somebody.
*You are **'phum jai'**.*

plaeg jai แปลกใจ **surprised**
If something surprises you, then you are
***'plaeg jai'** or also **'pralaat jai'**.*

pratap jai ประทับใจ **impressed**
Thailand impresses you.
*You are **'pratap jai'** with Thailand.*

saab sueng jai ซาบซึ้งใจ **grateful**
*You are lost in downtown Bangkok and can't find back to your hotel. A stranger helps you and shows you the way back. You feel **'saab sueng jai'** for this person.*

sabaai jai สบายใจ **happy**
You will hear this all the time.
It means happiness and satisfaction.

sao jai เศร้าใจ **broken heart, sad**
*This means broken heart. You feel sad, have no more interest in anything; you feel **'sao jai'**.*

sia jai เสียใจ **regret, sorrow**
*If you feel sorry for a person, you say **'sia jai'**.*

son jai สนใจ **interested**
You are interested in something or somebody.
You feel ***'son jai'.***

tat sin jai ตัดสินใจ **decide, decision**
This 'heart' word means decision.

thang jai ตั้งใจ **concentrate**
You are concentrating on what you are doing.
You put all your energy in a project.
You are ***'thang jai'.***

tok jai ตกใจ **frightened**
If you are frightened, you will feel ***'tok jai'.***

waan jai หวานใจ **darling, sweetheart**
This word has the meaning of darling.

wai jai ไว้ใจ **trust**
You trust somebody 100%. You have ***'wai jai'*** *to this person.*

Additional words

aarom = *mood, feeling* อารมณ์
aarom dee = *be in great mood* อารมณ์ดี
aarom sia = *be in bad mood* อารมณ์เสีย
aarom ngut ngit = *moody* อารมณ์หงุดหงิด

afraid	glua	กลัว
ambitious, diligent	khayan	ขยัน
angry, furious	grot, moho	โกรธ, โมโห
annoyed	ramkaan	รำคาญ
bored	bue-a	เบื่อ
brave, courageous	glaa haan	กล้าหาญ
cheerful	yindee	ยินดี
confused	sapson	สับสน
cowardly	mai glaa	ไม่กล้า
crazy	baa, prasaat	บ้า
curious	yaak roo yaak hen	อยากรู้อยากเห็น
disappointed	phit wang	ผิดหวัง
distrustful	song sai	สงสัย
envious	it chaa	อิจฉา
excited	tuen ten	ตื่นเต้น
false	khee gong	ขี้โกง
frustrated	gravon gravai	กระวนกระวาย
happy	mee kwaam suk	มีความสุข
jealous	hueng	หึง

joyful, cheerful	raa roeng	ร่าเริง
lazy	khee kiat	ขี้เกียจ
lonely	ngao	เหงา
lovesickness	ok hak	อกหัก
miserable, lousy	pen took	เป็นทุกข์
miss	khit thueng	คิดถึง
mourn, grieve	sok sao	โศกเศร้า
nervous	ngut ngit	หงุดหงิด
pity	songsaan	สงสาร
playful	khee len	ขี้เล่น
polite	suphaap	สุภาพ
sad	sao	เศร้า
shy	khee aai	ขี้อาย
stingy, mean	khee niaw	ขี้เหนียว
stubborn	due	ดื้อ
worried	gang won	กังวล
worry	pen huang	เป็นห่วง

mee nut gup = *date, rendezvous* มีนัดกับ
pit nut = *stand somebody up* ผิดนัด

ruk = *love* รัก
tok loom ruk = *fall in love* ตกหลุมรัก
ruk saam sao = *love triangle* รักสามเศร้า

'naa daeng' *= embarrassed* หน้าแดง
Thais like to laugh and will do so if
a small mishap will happen to you.
Don't get angry. Thais love fun.

'la aai' *= be ashamed* ละอาย
You feel embarrassed and bad
at the same time.
You are ashamed.

Examples: feelings

I like it (very much).

Chawp (maak).
ชอบ (มาก)

I am sad.

Sia jai.
เสียใจ

I don't like it so much.

Mai chawp maak.
ไม่ชอบมาก

Take it easy !

Jai yen yen !
ใจเย็นๆ

I hate that (very much).

Glee-at (maak).
เกลียด (มาก)

I am angry.

Moho.
โมโห

I am happy.

Mee kwaam suk.
มีความสุข

You made me angry.

Moho khun.
โมโหคุณ

How stupid !

Naa ram kaan !
น่ารำคาญ

That's typical for you !

Taang pee !
ทั้งปี

Oh, that's good !

Sabaai jai ! Long ok !
สบายใจ, โล่งอก

That's what you get for it !

Som naam naa !
สมน้ำหน้า

I am scared.

Glua.
กลัว

I am disappointed.

Pit wang.
ผิดหวัง

I am so worried.

Khit maak.
คิดมาก

Don't worry !

Mai tawng huang !
ไม่ต้องห่วง

That's so boring.

Bue-a. Seng.
เบื่อ, เซ็ง

Dream away.

Fun glang wun.
ฝันกลางวัน

Let me think about it.

Kho khit doo gon.
ขอคิดดูก่อน

I made a mistake.

Tham pit.
ทำผิด

I did this wrong.

Pit pai laew.
ผิดไปแล้ว

I am so angry, mad.

Aarom sia.
อารมณ์เสีย

Right ?

Tham thook rue plaao ?
ทำถูกหรือเปล่า

Wrong ?

Tham pit mai ?
ทำผิดไหม

Do you have a good time ? Are you happy ?

Mee kwaam suk rue plaao ?
มีความสุขหรือเปล่า

That's so boring.

Naa bue-a maak.
น่าเบื่อมาก

I am having a great time.

Phom sanuk maak.
ผมสนุกมาก

Never mind !

Mai pen rai !
ไม่เป็นไร

Cute.

Naa rak.
น่ารัก

Very smart.

Chalaad chang. Chalaad maak.
ฉลาดจัง, ฉลาดมาก

LOVE

Get to know each other...

Are you here alone ?

Khun maa khawn diaw rue plaao ?
คุณมาคนเดียวหรือเปล่า

Do you like something to drink ?

Khun tawng gaan duem arai mai ?
คุณต้องการดื่มอะไรไหม

May I sit here ?

Nang duai daai mai ?
นั่งด้วยได้ไหม

Somebody sits here already ?

Theenee mee khawn nang mai ?
ที่นี่มีคนนั่งไหม

What's your name ?

Khun chue arai ?
คุณชื่ออะไร

Where do you live ?

Baan khun yoo theenai ?
บ้านคุณอยู่ที่ไหน

Where do you come from ?

Khun maa chaak nai ?
คุณมาจากไหน

How old are you ?

Khun aayoo thaorai ?
คุณอายุเท่าไหร่

What do you work ?

Khun tham ngaan arai ?
คุณทำงานอะไร

Where do you work?

Khun tham ngaan theenai?
คุณทำงานที่ไหน

What do you do in your free time ?

Khun tham arai waelaa waang ?
คุณทำอะไรเวลาว่าง

Do you come here often ?

Khum maa theenee booi mai ?
คุณมาที่นี่บ่อยไหม

Did we meet before ?

Rao kooi phop gan rue plaao ?
เราเคยพบกันหรือเปล่า

What music do you like ?

Chawp dontree arai ?
ชอบดนตรีอะไร

What do you like ?

Khun chawp arai ?
คุณชอบอะไร

Do you know this song ?

Khun roo chak plaeng nee rue plaao ?
คุณรู้จักเพลงนี้หรือเปล่า

What's your favourite music ?

Khun chawp plaeng arai thee sut ?
คุณชอบเพลงอะไรที่สุด

That's my favourite song.

Plaeng nee pen plaeng ploot khawng chan.
เพลงนี้เป็นเพลงโปรดของฉัน

I will request it for you.

Phom cha khaw plaeng nee haai khun.
ผมจะขอเพลงนี้ให้คุณ

Would you like to dance with me?

Tenram duai gan mai ?
เต้นรำด้วยกันไหม

You dance very well.

Khun tenram geng maak.
คุณเต้นรำเก่งมาก

How did you find this place ?

Khun roo chak theenee daai yang ngai ?
คุณรู้จักที่นี่ได้ยังไง

My friends showed me.

Phuean bawk.
เพื่อนบอก

Where else do you usually go ?

Taa khun mai maa theenee khun cha pai theenai ?
ถ้าคุณไม่มาที่นี่คุณจะไปที่ไหน

Where is that ?

Theenai ?
ที่ไหน

Let us sit over there.

Pai nang theenan gan mai.
ปนั่งที่นั่นกันไหม

Don't you think it's too loud here ?

Khun khit waa theenee seeang dang pai rue plaao ?
คุณคิดว่าที่นี่เสียงดังไปหรือเปล่า

How long will you stay here ?

Khun cha yoo theenee eek naan thaorai ?
คุณจะอยู่ที่นี่อีกนานเท่าไหร่

It depends.

Laew tae.
แล้วแต่

If I am bored, I will go home.

Taa bue-a cha glup (baan).
ถ้าเบื่อจะกลับ (บ้าน)

If I have fun, I will stay here.

Taa sanuk cha yoo to.
ถ้าสนุกจะอยู่ต่อ

Should we go somewhere else ?

Pai thee uen gan mai ?
ไปที่อื่นกันไหม

What should we do next ?

Rao cha tham arai gan dee ton nee ?
เราจะทำอะไรกันดีตอนนี้

Up to you.

Laew tae khun.
แล้วแต่คุณ

Whatsoever.

Yangnai go daai. Arai go daai.
อย่างไหนก็ได้. อะไรก็ได้

Should we go already ?

Pai gan rue yung ?
ไปกันหรือยัง

Let's go !

Pai gan daai laew !
ไปกันได้แล้ว

I want to stay here longer.

Yaak yoo to eek nooi.
อยากอยู่ต่ออีกหน่อย

I will bring you home.

Phom cha song khun glup baan.
ผมจะส่งคุณกลับบ้าน

I want to know more about you.

Phom yaak roo chak khun maak kwaa nee.
ผมอยากรู้จักคุณมากกว่านี้

We think the same, don't we ?

Rao khit muean gan chai mai ?
เราคิดเหมือนกันใช่ไหม

Should we meet again ?

Rao cha phop gan eek mai ?
เราจะพบกันอีกไหม

When can I meet you again ?

Cha phop khun eek muearai ?
จะพบคุณอีกเมื่อไหร่

Can I have your telephone number ?

Khaw boe thorasap khun daai mai ?
ขอเบอร์โทรศัพท์คุณได้ไหม

Can I call you ?

Phom tho haa khun daai mai ?
ผมโทรหาคุณได้ไหม

See you soon.

Rao phop gan eek.
แล้วพบกันอีก

See you tomorrow.

Phop gan phrung nee.
พบกันพรุ่งนี้

Take care.

Doolae tua eng duai na.
ดูแลตัวเองด้วยนะ

Love stories

Love makes blind.

Kwaam ruk tham haai khawn taa bod.
ความรักทำให้คนตาบอด

I am crazy for you.

Phom/Chan klung klai nai tua khun.
ผม/ ฉันคลั่งใคล้ในตัวคุณ

I love you.

Phom/Chan ruk khun.
ผม/ฉันรักคุณ

You are beautiful.

Khun suai chang looi.
คุณสวยจังเลย

*The words **chang looi** will be added here often, but actually don't have a meaning.*

You are handsome.

Khun law chang looi.
คุณหล่อจังเลย

You are so cute.

Khun naa ruk chang looi.
คุณน่ารักจังเลย

You are sexy.

Khun seksee. Khun doo seksee chang looi.
คุณเซ็กซี่.คุณดูเซ็กซี่จังเลย

You have beautiful eyes.

Taa khun suai chang looi.
ตาคุณสวยจังเลย

You have a wonderful smile.

Khun yim suai chang looi.
คุณยิ้มสวยจังเลย

Flatterer !

Paak waan !
ปากหวาน

You are so quiet.

Khun ngiap chang looi.
คุณเงียบจังเลย

Can I kiss you ?

Choop nooi daai mai ? Khaw hom nooi daai mai ?
จูบหน่อยได้ไหม. ขอหอมหน่อยได้ไหม

Kiss me.

Choop/Hom daai.
จูบ/ หอมได้

hom = *kiss, peck*
to kiss somebody goodbye, otherwise
choop= *kiss*

Don't be shy.

Mai tawng aai.
ไม่ต้องอาย

Close your eyes.

Lap taa.
หลับตา

You have such a nice body, you are so sexy.

Khun mee roop raang suai ngaam.
คุณมีรูปร่างสวยงาม

Is this your first time ?

Khrung raek rue plaao ?
ครั้งแรกหรือเปล่า

Tell me the truth.

Bawk kwaam ching na.
บอกความจริงนะ

Don't be afraid.

Mai tawng khit maak.
ไม่ต้องคิดมาก

Do you have a condom ?

Khun mee tung yang anamaai (condom) mai ?
คุณมีถุงยางอนามัย (คอนดอม) ไหม

We should use a condom.

Sai kondom (tung yang anamaai) duai.
ใส่คอนดอม (ถุงยางอนามัย) ด้วย

Be tender to me.

Yaa run raeng na.
อย่ารุนแรงนะ

I feel so good.

Roosuek sabaai dee. Roosuek dee chang looi.
รู้สึกสบายดี. รู้สึกดีจังเลย

I don't want you go away from me.

Phom mai tawng gaan haai khun pai chaak phom.
ผมไม่ต้องการให้คุณไปจากผม

I want to stay with you.

Phom/Chan yaak yoo gup khun.
ผม/ฉันอยากอยู่กับคุณ

Farewell...

Will you send a letter ?

Khun chà khĭan chòtmăi thŭeng chăn rŭe plàao.
คุณจะเขียนจดหมายถึงฉันหรือเปล่า

I will send you a letter.

Phŏm chà khĭan chòtmăi thŭeng khun.
ผมจะเขียนจดหมายถึงคุณ

I will call you from England.

Phŏm chà tho hăa khun chàak ungkrit.
ผมจะโทรหาคุณจากอังกฤษ

I will come back soon.

Phŏm chà glùp maa rae-o rae-o née.
ผมจะกลับมาเร็วๆนี้

I have to leave because of my job.

Phŏm tâwng glùp pai tham ngaan.
ผมต้องกลับไปทำงาน

Wait until I come back.

Raw phŏm glùp maa ná.
รอผมกลับมานะ

Don't forget to write !

Yaa luem khian chotmai maa baang na !
อย่าลืมเขียนจดหมายมาบ้างนะ

Don't cry.

Yaa rong haai.
อย่าร้องไห้

Wipe your tears.

Chet naam taa.
เช็ดน้ำตา

I can't take it.

Phom/Chan ton mai daai.
ผม/ฉันทนไม่ได้

I miss you.

Khit thueng khun.
คิดถึงคุณ

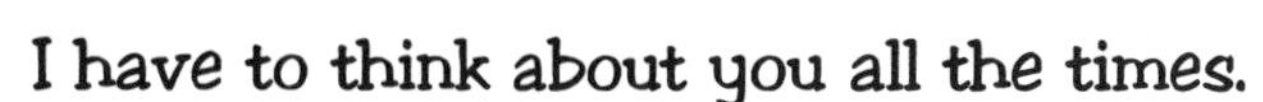

I have to think about you all the times.

Phom/Chan khit thueng khun samoe samoe.
ผม/ฉันคิดถึงคุณเสมอๆ

I will always love you.

Cha ruk khun talawt pai.
จะรักคุณตลอดไป

Take care.

Doolae tua eeng duai na.
ดูแลตัวเองด้วยนะ

Problems with the love life...

Please forgive me.

Yok thot haai daai mai.
ยกโทษให้ได้ไหม

I don't understand what's going on with you.

Phom mai roo waa goet arai khuen gup khun.
ผมไม่รู้ว่าเกิดอะไรขึ้นกับคุณ

Let me try to explain !

Khaw haai phom athibaai daai mai.
ขอให้ผมอธิบายได้ไหม

So explain it !

Athibaai maa see.
อธิบายมาสิ

I don't care.

Mai son jai. Chan mai kae.
ไม่สนใจ. ฉันไม่แคร์

This doesn't mean anything to me.

Mai mee kwaam maai samrap phom/chan. Mai kae.
ไม่มีความหมายสำหรับผม/ ฉัน. ไม่แคร์

This doesn't interest me.

Mai naa son jai.
ไม่น่าสนใจ.

I can't meet you anymore.

Phom/Chan phop khun eek mai daai laeo.
ผม/ ฉันพบคุณอีกไม่ได้แล้ว

I won't call you anymore.

Phom/Chan mai tho haa khun eek laeo.
ผม/ ฉันไม่โทรหาคุณอีกแล้ว

You don't love me anymore, do you ?

Khun mai ruk phom/chan eek laeo chai mai ?
คุณไม่รักผม/ ฉันอีกแล้วใช่ไหม

Do you have a new girlfriend (boyfriend) ?

Mee faen mai rue plaao ?
มีแฟนใหม่หรือเปล่า

Please tell me the truth.

Phoot kwaam ching.
พูดความจริง

I want to know.

Phom/Chan yaak roo.
ผม/ ฉันอยากรู้

I have a new girlfriend (boyfriend).

Phom/Chan mee faen mai laeo.
ผม/ ฉันมีแฟนใหม่แล้ว

I like you but I don't love you anymore.

Phom/Chan chawp khun tae phom/chan mai ruk khun eek laeo.
ผม/ ฉันชอบคุณแต่ผม/ ฉันไม่รักคุณอีกแล้ว

You don't interest me anymore.

Phom/Chan mai son jai khun eek laeo.
ผม/ ฉันไม่สนใจคุณอีกแล้ว

I don't have fun with you.

Yoo gup khun mai sanuk looi.
อยู่กับคุณไม่สนุกเลย

You are so boring.

Khun naa bue-a.
คุณน่าเบื่อ

You live behind the mountain !

Khun yoo lang khao !
คุณอยู่หลังเขา

I am so sorry that I can't be your girlfriend/boyfriend.

Phom/Chan sia jai phom/chan pen faen khun mai daai.
ผม/ฉันเสียใจ ผม/ฉันเป็นแฟนคุณไม่ได้

I feel so sorry !

Phom sia jai duai !
ผมเสียใจด้วย

It was my mistake.

Pen kwaam pit khong phom/chan eng.
เป็นความผิดของผม/ฉันเอง

It's nobody's mistake.

Mai mee khrai pit.
ไม่มีใครผิด

That's the way it is.

Arai cha goet go haai man goet.
อะไรจะเกิดก็ให้มันเกิด

Can we start again ?

Roem gan mai daai mai ?
เริ่มกันใหม่ได้ไหม

I am serious about you.

Phom/Chan ching chang gup khun na.
ผม/ฉันจริงจังกับคุณนะ

I can't live without you.

Yoo mai daai taa mai mee khun.
อยู่ไม่ได้ถ้าไม่มีคุณ

Do you understand my feelings to you ?

Khaojai kwaam roosuek khong phom/chan mai ?
เข้าใจความรู้สึกของผม/ฉันไหม

I will never forget you.

Phom/Chan cha mai luem khun.
ผม/ ฉันจะไม่ลืมคุณ

Thank you for this wonderful time.

Khawp khun samrap kwaam song cham thee dee.
ขอบคุณสำหรับความทรงจำที่ดี

I am so happy that I know you.

Phom/Chan mee kwaam suk thee daai roo chak khun.
ผม/ ฉันมีความสุขที่ได้รู้จักคุณ

Don't forget me.

Khit thueng phom/chan baang na.
คิดถึงผม/ฉันบ้างนะ

Can we be friends ?

Rao pen phuean gan daai mai ?
เราเป็นเพื่อนกันได้ไหม

See you in my next life !

Phop gan chaat naa !
พบกันชาติหน้า

Important PHRASES

What you will hear all the times !

1. mai pen rai ไม่เป็นไร **It doesn't matter !**
You will hear this phrase many times. You are in a traffic jam and miss your plane. You are desperate and upset. But you should relax and tell yourself ***'mai pen rai'****.*
Don't think Thais don't care. Don't misunderstand this phrase. Everybody just tries to cope with one's fate and tries to stay calm whatever happens. There is no point to get upset. The plane won't return.

2. jai yen yen ใจเย็นเย็น **calm, cool**
This phrase is widely used together with ***'mai pen rai'****. It means* ***'cool heart'****.*
Stay calm and don't get upset or lose your temper. If you get angry, you will hear ***'jai yen yen'****.*

3. sanuk สนุก **fun**
Thais love to have fun. They know how to entertain and having a good time.
Thais don't like to sit home alone. They enjoy going out together and having fun.
Even during a financial crisis everybody takes it easy and enjoys life as much as possible.
We are sure you will have lots of fun in Thailand and won't get bored.

4. sabaai สบาย **happy**

*You will get asked '**sabaai mai?**' many times. '**Sabaai**' means happy and satisfied and '**mai**' is the particle to form a question. You will most probable answer '**sabaai maak**' (=very happy).*

5. double words

*Sometimes you will hear some words repeated. This is done to emphasis. Words, which are widely used, are for example '**maak-maak**' (very much), '**ching - ching**' (100% sure), '**rae-o – rae-o**' (very fast), '**chaa – chaa**' (very slow) or also '**jai yen yen**' (cool heart).*

6. nicknames

*Most Thai people use nicknames instead of their real names. You will be surprised about some translations of these nicknames. These nicknames have meanings like '**rat**', '**pig**', '**sugar**' or even '**Pepsi**' like our Thai editor.*

*But don't forget to use the particle '**Khun**' (= Mr., Mrs., Miss) with these nicknames. If your nickname will be 'Fatty', don't get angry.*

7. rue plaao, laew rue yung หรือเปล่า, แล้วหรือยัง

*Some questions end with '**rue plaao**' or with '**laew rue yung**'. This has the meaning of 'or not ?' and 'already or not yet?'.*

8. chai mai ใช่ไหม

*Other questions end with '**chai mai**'. This can be translated with 'is it, isn't it'.* *(see also chapter question & answer, pages 38-43)*

9. daai mai ได้ไหม

*Many questions end with '**daai mai**'. '**daai**' means 'to be able, can' and '**mai**' is the particle to form a question.*

10. riap rooi เรียบร้อย **ready, okay**

*The question '**riap rooi laew ?**' means' **Is everything ready, okay ?**'.*

EVERYDAY CONVERSATION

Common phrases...

What's your name ?

Khun chue arai ?
คุณชื่ออะไร

Where do you live ?

Baan yoo nai ?
บ้านอยู่ไหน

Where do you come from ?

Khun maa chaak nai ?
คุณมาจากไหน

How old are you ?

Khun aayoo thaorai ?
คุณอายุเท่าไหร่

What are you doing in your spare time ?

Khun tham arai waelaa waang ?
คุณทำอะไรเวลาว่าง

Are you already a long time in Thailand ?

Khun yoo muang Thai naan laeo rue yung ?
คุณอยู่เมืองไทยนานแล้วหรือยัง

Do you like Thai girls ?

Chawp phooying Thai mai ?
ชอบผู้หญิงไทยไหม

You look younger / older than you are.

Khun doo oon / gae kwaa aayoo.
คุณดูอ่อน / แก่กว่าอายุ

See you soon again.

Laeo phop gan mai.
แล้วพบกันใหม่

See you tomorrow.

Phrung nee phop gan mai.
พรุ่งนี้พบกันใหม่

What are you thinking ?

Khun gamlang khit arai yoo ?
คุณกำลังคิดอะไรอยู่

Nothing !

Plaao !
เปล่า

Sure ?

Ching ? Ching-ching ? Ching rue plaao ?
จริง/ จริงๆ/ จริงหรือเปล่า

You must be joking, are you joking ?

Phoot len chai mai ?
พูดเล่นใช่ไหม

You are leading me up the garden path, aren't you !

Khun gohok phom/chan chai mai !
คุณโกหกผม/ ฉันใช่ไหม

Is that for certain ?

Nae jai mai ?
แน่ใจไหม

I don't believe that.

Mai chuea.
ไม่เชื่อ

That's right !

Chai ! Chai laeo !
ใช่/ ใช่แล้ว

There is something wrong here.

Mai thook.
ไม่ถูก

So much is certain !

Nae non !
แน่นอน

I bet on it.

Panan daai loei.
พนันได้เลย

Of course !

Daai see !
ได้สิ

I am not sure about it.

Mai nae jai.
ไม่แน่ใจ

Maybe ! Perhaps !

Baang thee !
บางที

That's my idea of it !

Phom/Chan khit yung nee !
ผม/ ฉันคิดอย่างนี้

That's impossible to find out.

Mai mee thaang roo.
ไม่มีทางรู้

Can you do that ?

Khun tham yung nan daai mai ?
คุณทำอย่างนั้นได้ไหม

I can't possibly do it.

Tham mai daai.
ทำไม่ได้

Can't you do that ?

Khun tham daai rue plaao ?
คุณทำได้หรือเปล่า

I will try to do that.

Phom cha long tham.
ผมจะลองทำ

I see ! I got it ! I understand !

Khao jai laeo.
เข้าใจแล้ว

Never ! Impossible !

Mai mee thaang !
ไม่มีทาง

I think the same.

Khit muean gan.
คิดเหมือนกัน

Okay ! All right !

Toklong !
ตกลง

No problem.

Mai mee panhaa.
ไม่มีปัญหา

Do you know ?

Roo rue plaao ?
รู้หรือเปล่า

Oh, you know that !

Khun roo laeo law !
คุณรู้แล้วเหรอ

I didn't know that.

Yung mai roo.
ยังไม่รู้

Meeting friends

What's going on ? What's up ?

Pen yung ngai (baang) ?
เป็นยังไง(บ้าง)

Nothing doing around here !

Mai mee arai !
ไม่มีอะไร

What happened ?

Goet arai khuen ?
เกิดอะไรขึ้น

What's going on today ?

Wan nee mee arai peeset mai ?
วันนี้มีอะไรพิเศษไหม

Nothing special !

Mai mee arai peeset !
ไม่มีอะไรพิเศษ

How are you ?

Sabaai dee na ?
สบายดีนะ

So and so (fifty - fifty).

haa sip - haa sip
ห้าสิบ-ห้าสิบ

What are doing just now ?

Khun gamlang tham arai yoo ?
คุณกำลังทำอะไรอยู่

What did you do all the time ?

Khun pai tham arai maa ?
คุณไปทำอะไรมา

Where have you been all the time ?

Khun painai maa ?
คุณไปไหนมา

It was a long time ago we have met !

Mai daai phop gan naan laeo na !
ไม่ได้พบกันนานแล้วนะ

I beg your pardon ?

Pardon ? I didn't get that.

Phom fang mai tan.
ผมฟังไม่ทัน

Listen !

Fang ! Fang see ! Fang na !
ฟัง/ ฟังสิ/ ฟังนะ

Listen first !

Fang gon !
ฟังก่อน

Do you listen to me ?

Daai yin phom/chan phoot mai ?
ได้ยินผม/ ฉันพูดไหม

I couldn't hear you.

Mai daai yin loei.
ไม่ได้ยินเลย

I don't want to hear it.

Mai yaak daai yin.
ไม่อยากได้ยิน

Say something !

Phoot arai baang see !
พูดอะไรบ้างสิ

I don't want to speak.

Mai tawng gaan phoot arai.
ไม่ต้องการพูดอะไร

What are you talking about ?

Khun phoot rueang arai ?
คุณพูดเรื่องอะไร

What did you say ?

Khun gamlang phoot arai yoo ?
คุณกำลังพูดอะไรอยู่

What do you mean by that ?

Maai kwaam waa arai ?
หมายความว่าอะไร

You shouldn't say that !

Khun mai khuan phoot yung nee !
คุณไม่ควรพูดอย่างนี้

You said that, didn't you ?

Khun phoot yung nan chai mai ?
คุณพูดอย่างนั้นใช่ไหม

I didn't say that !

Phom/Chan mai daai phoot yung nan !
ผม / ฉันไม่ได้พูดอย่างนั้น

I didn't say anything !

Mai daai phoot arai loei !
ไม่ได้พูดอะไรเลย

I didn't mean it like that !

Mai daai maai kwaam waa yung nan !
ไม่ได้หมายความว่าอย่างนั้น

Lame excuse !

Mai toong gae tua !
ไม่ต้องแก้ตัว

Do you know what you are talking about ?

Khun phoot arai pai ?
คุณพูดอะไรไป

Don't shout !

Yaa phoot seeang dang !
อย่าพูดเสียงดัง

Not so loud.

Phoot baw baw nooi.
พูดเบาๆหน่อย

Don't talk so fast.

Phoot chaa chaa nooi.
พูดช้าๆหน่อย

Say again.

Phoot eek khrung.
พูดอีกครั้ง

Look !

Look !

Mong nee see ! Mong doo ! Doo see !
มองนี่สิ/มองดู/ดูสิ

mong *or* ***mong doo :*** *look at*

Look at that !

Mong thee nee ! Doo thee nee !
มองที่นี่/ ดูที่นี่

doo : *watch*
(e.g. watch a movie)

Don't look !

Yaa mong na !
อย่ามองนะ

Did you see that ?

Hen mai ?
เห็นไหม

hen : *see something or somebody*

I saw it.

Hen laeo.
เห็นแล้ว

I didn't see it.

Mai koei hen.
ไม่เคยเห็น

I couldn't see it.

Mong mai hen.
มองไม่เห็น

mong hen : see, notice

I don't want to see it.

Mai yaak hen.
ไม่อยากเห็น

mong haa : look for, search for

Show me !

Khaw doo nooi !
ขอดูหน่อย

Let me see first !

Khaw doo gon !
ขอดูก่อน

haa : look around for (e.g. I am looking around for a new house = phom haa baan mai)

I will show you.

Cha haai khun doo.
จะให้คุณดู

Slang

Be careful with the following phrases !
Some of these words can be offensive and rude.

What's your problem ?!

Mee panhaa arai ?!
มีปัญหาอะไร

What do you want ?!

Khun cha aw arai ?!
คุณจะเอาอะไร

That's none of your business !

Mai chai thura khawng khun na !
ไม่ใช่ธุระของคุณนะ

Do you want to say something ?

Khun yaak cha phoot arai ?
คุณอยากจะพูดอะไร

What did you say ?

Khun phoot arai ?
คุณพูดอะไร

Why do you talk like that ?

Thammai khun phoot yung nee ?!
ทำไมคุณพูดอย่างนี้

Don't talk nonsense !

Yaa phoot arai ngo ngo !
อย่าพูดอะไรโง่ๆ

That's a lie !

Khun phoot gohok !
คุณพูดโกหก

Don't lie !

Yaa gohok na !
อย่าโกหกนะ

Forget it ! That's enough !

Mai aw ! Paw laeo !
ไม่เอา/ พอแล้ว

That should be enough now !

Khuan cha paw laeo !
ควรจะพอแล้ว

Such nonsense !

Tolae !
ตอแหล

Don't stare at me !

Yaa mong chan na !
อย่ามองฉันนะ

What are you doing ?

Khun tham arai ?!
คุณทำอะไร

Stupid ! You are so silly !

Ngo ! Khun pen khon ngo !
โง่/ คุณเป็นคนโง่

You are crazy, mad !

Khun prasaat !
คุณประสาท

Don't behave like an idiot !

Yaa tham arai ngo ngo !
อย่าทำอะไรโง่ๆ

Stop it !

Yut !
หยุด

Don't do something like that !

Yaa tham yung nee !
อย่าทำอย่างนี้

Why do you do something like that ?

Thammai khun tham yung nee ?
ทำไมคุณทำอย่างนี้

Leave me alone !

Khaw haai chan yoo khon diaw !
ขอให้ฉันอยู่คนเดียว

Leave her alone !

Haai khao yoo khon diaw !
ให้เขาอยู่คนเดียว

Do what I tell you !

Tham yung thee phom bawk !
ทำอย่างที่ผมบอก

Come here !

Maa nee see !
มานี่สิ

You make a lot of noise !

Khun seeang dang goen pai laeo !
คุณเสียงดังเกินไปแล้ว

Shut up!

Yaa phoot ! Hub paak !
อย่าพูด/ หุบปาก

Be quiet !

Ngiap !
เงียบ

Liar ! Maniac !

Gohok ! Tolae !
โกหก/ ตอแหล

Show-off !

Paak maak !
ปากมาก

Playboy !

Chao shoo !
เจ้าชู้

Coward ! Sissy !

Ai naa tua mia !
ไอ้หน้าตัวเมีย

Alcoholic ! Boozer ! Drunkard !

Khee maw.
ขี้เมา

Meanie !

Khee niaw !
ขี้เหนียว

Lecher !

Ta lueng !
ทะลึ่ง

Don't get on my nerves !

Yaa yung !
อย่ายุ่ง

Get out !

Ok pai glai glai !
ออกไปไกลๆ

Get lost !

Pai loei !
ไปเลย

Who do you think you are ?

Khun khit waa khun pen khrai ?
คุณคิดว่าคุณเป็นใคร

Do you want to fool me ?

Khee gong rue plaao ?
ขี้โกงหรือเปล่า

Why is it so expensive ?

Thammai phaeng maak ?
ทำไมแพงมาก

Is it so expensive because I am a tourist ?

Phaeng phro waa phom pen khon farang chai mai ?
แพงเพราะว่าผมเป็นคนฝรั่งใช่ไหม

Don't think I am stupid !

Yaa khit waa phom pen khon ngo !
อย่าคิดว่าผมเป็นคนโง่

I will report this to the police !

Phom bawk tamruat na !
ผมบอกตำรวจนะ

'THAI -- ENGLISH'

English language ?

Thais like to use words from the English language.
However, sometimes these 'English' words sound quite different to the original.
The more imagination you have the easier to understand.

We listed a few words you most probably will hear.

apartment	aapaatmen	อพาร์ทเม้นต์
bank	baenk	แบ็งค์
bar	baa	บาร์
battery	baetaaree	แบตเตอร์รี่
beer bar	baa biar	บาร์ เบียร์
bus	bas	บัส
computer	compjutaa	คอมพิวเตอร์
disco	disako	ดิสโก้
fashion	faeshan	แฟชั่น
football	futbon	ฟุตบอล
free	fee	ฟรี
furniture	foerni shoer	เฟอร์นิเจอร์
honeymoon	haneemoon	ฮันนีมูน
hotel	hoten	โฮเต็ล
idea	aidee-aa	ไอเดีย
lipstick	lipsatik	ลิปสติค
motorcycle	mootoersaik	มอเตอร์ไซค์
postcard	pot kaat	โปสการ์ด

problem	plomplem	พลอมแพลม
romantic	romaantik	โรมานติก
serious	seeleeat	ซีเรียส
shopping	chop ping	ช้อปปิ้ง
shopping plaza	chop ping phlaasaa	ช้อปปิ้งพลาซ่า
six	sik	ซิค
spaghetti	sapaagetee	สปาเกตตี้
stamp	sa taem	แสตมป์
steak	sataek	สเต็ก
sure	shuaa	ชัวร์
taxi	taeksee	แท็กซี่
town house	thaon hao	ทาวน์เฮาส์
video	weedeo	วีดีโอ

Do you play golf ?

Up-to-date information on all golf resorts in Thailand !

RESTAURANT and BAR

Useful words

raan aahaan = *smaller restaurant* ร้านอาหาร
pataakaan = *bigger restaurant* ภัตตาคาร

aahaan = *food* อาหาร
aahaan chaao = *breakfast* อาหารเช้า
aahaan glaang wun = *lunch* อาหารกลางวัน
aahaan yen = *dinner* อาหารเย็น
aahaan kam = *late night snack* อาหารค่ำ

hiw naam = *thirsty* หิวน้ำ
hiw kaao = *hungry* หิวข้าว

ashtray	thee khia buree	ที่เขี่ยบุหรี่
bottle	kuat	ขวด
bottle opener	thee poet kuat	ที่เปิดขวด
bowl	chaam	ชาม
chair	gaoee	เก้าอี้
chopsticks	takiap	ตะเกียบ
cigarettes	buree	บุหรี่
pack of cigarettes	song buree	ซองบุหรี่
corkscrew, wine opener	thee poet chook wine	ที่เปิดจุกไวน์
cup	tuay	ถ้วย

drink	duem	ดื่ม
eat	kin kaao, thaan kaao	กินข้าว, ทานเข้า
food	aahaan	อาหาร
fork	som	ซ้อม
glass	gaew	แก้ว
knife	meet	มีด
lighter	fai chaek	ไฟแช็ค
market	talaat	ตลาด
matches	maai kheet fai	ไม้ขีดไฟ
menu	menyu	เมนู
napkin	gradaat, phaa chet paak	กระดาษ, ผ้าเช็ดปาก
plate	chaan	จาน
smoking	soob buree	สูบบุหรี่
spoon	chon	ช้อน
service, waiter	dek soef aahaan	เด็กเสริฟอาหาร
table	to	โต๊ะ
tablecloth	phaa poo to	ผ้าปูโต๊ะ
toothpick	maay chim fun	ไม้จิ้มฟัน

Drinks

drink, beverage	khrueang duem	เครื่องดื่ม
alcoholic beverage	laao	เหล้า
beer	bia	เบียร์
water	naam, naam plaao	น้ำ, น้ำเปล่า
boiled water	naam tom	น้ำต้ม
ice cubes, ice	naam kaeng	น้ำแข็ง
coffee (hot or cold)	kaafae	กาแฟ
coffee (hot, milk & sugar)	kaafae rawn	กาแฟร้อน
coffee (hot, no milk, no sugar)	kaafae dam	กาแฟดำ
iced coffee (milk & sugar)	kaafae yen	กาแฟเย็น
iced coffee (no milk, sugar)	o liang	โอเลี้ยง

mai sai naam taan = without sugar ไม่ใส่น้ำตาล

aw waan waan = sweet เอาหวานๆ

aw nom maak maak = with a lot of milk เอานมมากๆ

milk	nom	นม
soy milk	naam tao hoo	น้ำเต้าหู้
ovaltine	owantin	โอวัลติน
yoghurt	nom priaaw	นมเปรี้ยว

tea (hot or cold)	chaa	ชา
tea (hot, milk & sugar)	chaa rawn	ชาร้อน
tea (hot, milk, no sugar)	chaa dam rawn	ชาดำร้อน
iced tea (milk & sugar)	chaa yen	ชาเย็น
iced tea (no milk, sugar)	chaa dam yen	ชาดำเย็น
light tea	naam chaa	น้ำชา
Chinese tea	chaa chin	ชาจีน
tea leaf	bai chaa	ใบชา

naam + name of the fruit = *fruit juice*
e.g: ***naam sapparot*** = *pineapple juice*

fruit juice	naam ponlamaai	น้ำผลไม้
fruit juice (with crushed ice)	naam ponlamaai pan	น้ำผลไม้ปั่น
fresh squeezed orange juice	naam som kan	น้ำส้มคั้น
lime juice (with sugar, also salt)	naam manaao	น้ำมะนาว

pan = *Add this word and you will get your fresh fruit juice mixed with crushed ice.*

In Thailand one adds a little bit of salt to fresh fruit juices. If you would like to have your fruit juice without any salt, you say:
mai sai gluea ไม่ใส่เกลือ

Fruits

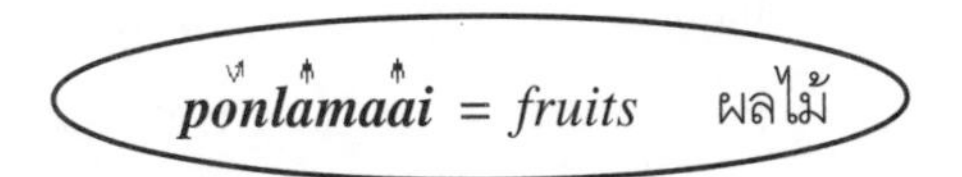

apple	aeppen	แอปเปิ้ล
banana	kluai	กล้วย
banana (long, sweet)	kluai hom	กล้วยหอม
banana (thick, sweet)	kluai naam waa	กล้วยน้ำหว้า
banana (small, sweet)	kluai kai	กล้วยไข่
banana (slightly süß)	kluai taanee	กล้วยตานี
banana (with pips)	kluai hak muk	กล้วยหักมุก
bel fruit	matoom	มะตูม
coconut	mapraao	มะพร้าว
durian	turian	ทุเรียน
gooseberry	mayom	มะยม
granat apple	taptim	ทับทิม
grape	angun	องุ่น
guava	farang	ฝรั่ง
jackfruit	khanun	ขนุน
langsat	langsat	ลางสาด
lime	manaao	มะนาว
longan	lamyai	ลำใย
lychee	linchee	ลิ้นจี่
mango	mamuang	มะม่วง
mangosteen	mangkut	มังคุด

melon	taeng tai	แตงไทย
orange	som	ส้ม
papaya	malako	มะละกอ
pear	pae	แพร์
pineapple	sapparot	สับปะรด
pomelo	som-o	ส้มโอ
rambeh	mafai	มะไฟ
rambutan	ngo	เงาะ
roseapple	chomphoo	ชมพู่
santol	graton	กระท้อน
sapodilla	lamut	ละมุด
star apple	ma fueang	มะเฟือง
sugarapple	nooi naa	น้อยหน่า
tamarind	makaam	มะขาม
watermelon	taeng mo	แตงโม

Cooking terms

tham kap kaao = *cook* ทำกับข้าว

bake	op	อบ
boil	tom	ต้ม
chopped	sap	สับ
deep fry	tot	ทอด
fry	pat	ผัด
fry (without sauce)	kua	คั่ว
grill	yaang, paao	ย่าง, เผา
raw	dip	ดิบ
stew, steam	nueng	นึ่ง
toast	ping	ปิ้ง
(well) done	suk	สุก

Taste & Flavour

rot = *flavour* รส
chim = *to taste* ชิม

bitter	kom	ขม
crisp	krawp	กรอบ
salty	kem	เค็ม
sour	preeaw	เปรี้ยว
spicy, hot	phet	เผ็ด
sweet	waan	หวาน
sweet & sour	preeaw - waan	เปรี้ยว - หวาน
tasteless	chuet	จืด

Spices

cooking oil	naam mun	น้ำมัน
pepper	prik thai	พริกไท
salt	glue-a	เกลือ
sauce	saws	ซอส
sugar	naam taan	น้ำตาล
vinegar	naam som sai choo	น้ำส้มสายชู

Thai spices

naam cheem น้ำจิ้ม

sauce -- on nearly every table in all restaurants

naam som prik dawng น้ำส้มพริกดอง

vinegar--with chilli

naam plaa น้ำปลา

fisch sauce -- is used instead of salt

prik naam plaa พริกน้ำปลา

fisch sauce -- with chilli

kapee กะปิ

shrimp paste -- made from very tiny shrimps

naam prik kapee น้ำพริกกะปิ

shrimp sauce -- spicy

sos prik ซอสพริก

chilli sauce -- similar to ketchup, but spicy, with tomatos, garlic and chilli

naam prik num น้ำพริกหนุ่ม

chilli sauce -- from Northern Thailand, spicy, green colour

prik paao พริกเผา

chilli -- chopped and roasted chillies

naam prik paao น้ำพริกเผา

chilli paste – from *prik paao*, garlic, onions and *naam plaa*

prik pon พริกป่น

chilli powder

seeyoo khaao / seeyoo dum ซีอิ้วขาว/ ซีอิ้วดำ

soy sauce -- called black or white soy sauce, but both are black in colour

naam mun hooi น้ำมันหอย

oyster sauce -- is used for cooking

Breakfast

egg	khai	ไข่
boiled eggs	khai tom	ไข่ต้ม
half boiled eggs	khai luak	ไข่ลวก
plain omelet	khai chiaw	ไข่เจียว
stuffed omelet	khai yat sai	ไข่ยัดไส้
scrambled eggs	khai kon	ไข่คน
fried eggs	khai dao	ไขดาว่
bread	kanom pang	ขนมปัง
butter	nooi	เนย
jam, marmalade	yam	แยม
honey	naam pueng	น้ำผึ้ง

Small snacks

gap glaem = *snack* กับแกล้ม

shrimp chips	kaao kriap kung	ข้าวเกรียบกุ้ง
potato chips	man farang tot	มันฝรั่งทอด
cashew nuts	met mamuang tot	เม็ดมะม่วงทอด
peanuts	tua tot	ถั่วทอด
fish cake	toot man plaa	ทอดมันปลา
roasted eggs	khai ping	ไข่ปิ้ง
meat balls	look chin ping	ลูกชิ้นปิ้ง
hot dog	sai krog	ไส้กรอก
spring roll	po pia tot	ปอเปี๊ยะทอด
satay	sate	สะเต๊ะ
spare ribs	see krong moo tot	ซี่โครงหมูทอด

Salads

yum *= Thai salad -- delicious, but very spicy. Is eaten as first course or small snack in the bar.*

beef salad	yum nuea	ยำเนื้อ
glass noodle salad	yum wunsen	ยำวุ้นเส้น
mango salad	yum mamuang	ยำมะม่วง
mixed salad	yum ruam mit	ยำรวมมิตร
pomelo salad	yum som-o	ยำส้มโอ
prawn salad	yum kung	ยำกุ้ง
seafood salad	yum ruam mit thalae	ยำรวมมิตรทะเล
squid salad	yum plaa muek	ยำปลาหมึก
sausage salad	yum sai krog	ยำไส้กรอก
sausage spread	yum moo yo	ยำหมูยอ

***lub** = Thai salad -- cooked and chopped, spicy, from Isaan (North-East Thailand)*

duck salad	lub pet	ลาบเป็ด
chicken salad	lub gai	ลาบไก่
beef salad	lub nuea	ลาบเนื้อ
pork salad	lub moo	ลาบหมู

***som tam** = papaya salad --*
made from green papaya, lemon, sugar, fish sauce, tomato, garlic, tiny tried shrimps or crab and lots of chillies.
Very spicy !

Soups

kaao tom *= rice soup -- eaten for breakfast, with different ingredients available.* ข้าวต้ม

chok *= rice porridge -- similar to 'kaao tom', but thicker.* โจ๊ก

Examples for different rice soups or rice porridges:

fish	kaao tom plaa	ข้าวต้มปลา
shrimps	kaao tom kung	ข้าวต้มกุ้ง
chicken	kaao tom gai	ข้าวต้มไก่
pork	kaao tom moo	ข้าวต้มหมู

guaitiaw naam *= noodle soup* ก๋วยเตี๋ยว

Following types of noodles are available:

sen yai *= thick noodles* เส้นใหญ่

sen lek *= thin noodles* เส้นเล็ก

sen mee *= very thin noodles* เส้นหมี่

ba mee *= egg noodles* บะหมี่

geeaw *= wonton* เกี๊ยว

guaitiaw naam sen yai look chin moo ก๋วยเตี๋ยวน้ำเส้นใหญ่ลูกชิ้นหมู

Soup with thick noodles and meat balls (=look chin) from pork (=muu)

guaitiaw naam sen lek look chin nuea ก๋วยเตี๋ยวน้ำเส้นเล็กลูกชิ้นเนื้อ

Soup with thin noodles and meat balls (=look chin) from beef (=nuea)

guaitiaw naam sen mee tap ก๋วยเตี๋ยวน้ำเส้นหมี่ตับ

Soup with very thin noodles and liver (=tap), pork or beef

ba mee geeaw naam moo daeng บะหมี่เกี๊ยวน้ำหมูแดง

Soup with egg noodles, wonton and 'red' prok meat

You can also order all noodle dishes without soup.

***Soups** are available everywhere in Thailand: from the exclusive restaurant to the hawker on the street. Above mentioned dishes are just a few of many more available.*
Many restaurants or food stalls are mostly specialized on only a few or even only one type of noodle soup variety.
Try them all - These soups are delicious and inexpensive !

*The **condiments (= khrueang prung)*** เครื่องปรุง *are on the table.*

***tom yum** = spicy - sour - soup*
probably the Thai national dish

tom yum kung ต้มยำกุ้ง

prawn soup – spicy, with lemon grass

tom yum paw taek, paw taek ต้มยำโป๊ะแตก, โป๊ะแตก

seafood soup -- with mussels, prawns, crabs, fish, etc.

***tom yum** is also available with chicken, different kinds of fish or other seafood varieties.*

More soups

tom kaa gai ต้มข่าไก่

chicken soup --similar to *'tom yum'*, with coconut milk

tom chuet wunsen moo sup ต้มจืดวุ้นเส้นหมูสับ

vegetable soup -- with chopped & minced pork (= moo sup) and glass noodles

tom chuet plaa muek yat sai ต้มจืดปลาหมึกยัดไส้

vegetable soup -- with stuffed squid and glass noodles

tom som plaa ต้มส้มปลา

fish soup -- sour & spicy

Curry

kaeng *= curry*

kaeng karee gai แกงกะหรี่ไก่

curry -- with coconut milk and chicken

kaeng khiaw waan moo แกงเขียวหวานหมู

curry -- green, sweet-sour curry with pork

kaeng som kung แกงส้มกุ้ง

curry -- sour & spicy, without coconut milk, with shrimps and vegetables

kaeng panaeng nuea แกงแพนงเนื้อ

curry -- thick curry with coconut milk and beef

kaeng phet gai แกงเผ็ดไก่

curry – spicy, with red chillies and chicken

kaeng liang แกงเลียง

curry -- with vegetables, chilli, thin

ho mok thalae ห่อหมกทะเล

seafood curry -- thick, with coconut milk, steamed in banana leaves

Rice dishes

kaao = *rice* ข้าว
kaao niaw = *sticky rice* ข้าวเหนียว

Rice is the main constituent in Thai food and there is an enormous varity of dishes with rice. Most dishes are served with rice and topped with chicken, pork, etc. Following a few typical dishes:

kaao mun gai ข้าวมันไก่

chicken on rice -- thin cut chicken meat on rice with chicken soup

kaao mok gai ข้าวหมกไก่

curry rice -- yellow curry rice with chicken and spicy soup

kaao moo daeng ข้าวหมูแดง

pork on rice -- red pork meat on rice

kaao moo krawp ข้าวหมูกรอบ

rice and pork -- crispy pork and rice

kaao nuea op ข้าวเนื้ออบ

rice with beef -- stove-fried beef on rice

kaao kluk kapee ข้าวคลุกกะปิ

rice -- fried with *'kapee'* sauce and egg, sweet pork meat and shrimps

kaao raat kaeng gai ข้าวราดแกงไก่

rice -- with chicken curry

Pasta

guaitiaw = *noodles* ก๋วยเตี๋ยว

sen yai = *thick noodles* เส้นใหญ่

sen lek = *thin noodles* เส้นเล็ก

sen mee = *very thin noodles* เส้นหมี่

ba mee = *egg noodles* บะหมี่

geeaw = *wonton* เกี๊ยว

wunsen = *glass noodles* วุ้นเส้น

guaitiaw haeng ก๋วยเตี๋ยวแห้ง

noodles without soup (see SOUPS, page 203-205 for different ingredients)

guaitiaw ruea ก๋วยเตี๋ยวเรือ

'boat noodles' = noodles, beef, species and black sauce

pat tai ผัดไทย

fried noodles - *'sen lek'* fried with prawns, vegetables, eggs and peanuts

pat seeyoo ผัดซีอิ๊ว

noodles with soy sauce - *'sen yai'* fried with black soy sauce

kanom cheen naam yaa ขนมจีนน้ำยา

noodles with fish curry

mee krawp หมี่กรอบ

crisp noodles -- crispy fried noodles with prawns and bean sprouts

raat naa ราดหน้า

noodles with thick sauce

Seafood

aahaan thalae = seafood อาหารทะเล

fish	plaa	ปลา
cod	plaa gao	ปลาเก๋า
eel	plaa lai	ปลาลาย
mackarel	plaa too	ปลาทู
perch	plaa kapong	ปลากะพง
shark	plaa chalaam	ปลาฉลาม
tuna	plaa o	ปลาโอ
squid	plaa muek	ปลาหมึก
white pomfret	plaa chalamet khaao	ปลาจะระเม็ดขาว
oyster	hooi naang rom	หอยนางรม
cockle	hooi kraeng	หอยแครง
mussels	hooi malaeng poo	หอยแมลงภู่
clams	hooi lai	หอยลาย
river crab	kang	กั้ง
crab	poo	ปู
prawn	kung	กุ้ง
lobster	kung mang gon	กุ้งมังกร
tiger prawn	kung gam gaam	กุ้งก้ามกาม

Seafood dishes

Thailand offers a wide variety in different seafood dishes. Many seafood restaurants will display the whole fish and shellfish sortiment on ice and you just choose what you like and how you would like to have it done.
Following some typical seafood dishes:

plaa preeaw waan ปลาเปรี้ยวหวาน

fish -- sweet & sour, with tomatos, pineapple, etc.

plaa tot ปลาทอด

fish -- fried fish, dipping sauce

plaa nueng manaao ปลานึ่งมะนาว

fish -- steamed in lime sauce and chillies

plaa nueng pae sa ปลานึ่งแป๊ะซะ

fish -- steamed with mushrooms and coriander

plaa raat prik ปลาราดพริก

fish -- fried with chilli dressing

plaa muek yat sai ปลาหมึกยัดไส้

squid -- filled with minced pork meat

hooi lai pat naam prik paao หอยลายผัดน้ำพริกเผา

clams -- fried in chilli sauce

hooi tot หอยทอด

mussels -- batter fried

hooi naang rom sot หอยนางรมสด

oyster -- on ice, with lime and onions

hooi malaeng poo op mo din หอยแมลงภู่อบหม้อดิน

mussels -- steamed, chilli sauce for dipping

kung paao กุ้งเผา

prawns -- grilled, chilli sauce for dipping

kung chup paeng tot กุ้งชุบแป้งทอด

prawns -- fried

kung chai naam plaa กุ้งแช่น้ำปลา

shrimps --raw, with garlic, lime and chilli sauce

kung nueng kratiam ton กุ้งนึ่งกระเทียมโทน

shrimps -- steamed with garlic

kung op wunsen กุ้งอบวุ้นเส้น

shrimps -- steamed and baked with soy sauce, with glass noodles

kung mang gon pat naam prik paao กุ้งมังกรผัดน้ำพริกเผา

lobster -- fried with chilli sauce

gaam poo nueng ก้ามปูนึ่ง

crab -- steamed, chilli sauce for dipping

Dishes - quick and easy

Listed below you will find some more very typical Thai dishes which you can order in nearly every restaurant.

Thai cooking is on of the very best, but please don't forget that many Thai dishes are very spicy !

kaao pat kung ข้าวผัดกุ้ง

fried rice -- with shrimps; also available with pork, chicken or crab meat. Very popular with travelers in Thailand.

gai pat met mamuang him ma paan ไก่ผัดเม็ดมะม่วงหิมพานต์

chicken -- fried with cashew nuts

gai pat king ไก่ผัดขิง

chicken -- fried with ginger and mushrooms

gai pat nomai ไก่ผัดหน่อไม้

chicken -- fried with bamboo sprouts

gai pat bai gaprao ไก่ผัดใบกะเพรา

chicken -- stir-fried with basil and chilli

gai pat nomai farang ไก่ผัดหน่อไม้ฝรั่ง

chicken -- fried with asparagus

nuea pat naam man hooi เนื้อผัดน้ำมันหอย

beef -- fried in oyster sauce

moo pat kratiam prik thai หมูผัดกระเทียมพริกไทย

pork -- fried with garlic and pepper

moo pat preeao waan หมูผัดเปรี้ยวหวาน

pork -- sweet & sour

kung pat naam prik paao กุ้งผัดน้ำพริกเผา

prawns -- fried in roasted chillies

poo pat bong galee ปูผัดผงกะหรี่

crab -- fried with cauliflower

pat pak ruam mit ผัดผักรวมมิตร

vegetable -- stir-fried for a short time

Sweets

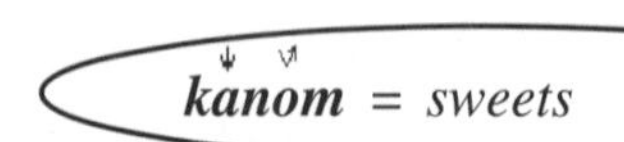

sang kayaa สังขยา

pudding -- made from pumpkin, eggs, sugar and coconut cream

sang kayaa mapraao สังขยามะพร้าว

pudding -- same as above, served in a coconut

sang kayaa fak toong สังขยาฟักทอง

pudding -- in a pumpkin

naam kaeng sai น้ำแข็งใส

sweets -- sugar peas, beans, potatos, sticky rice, fruits, coconut cream, crushed ice

fooi tong ฝอยทอง

egg yolk -- fried in sweet syrup

tong yod ทองหยอด

egg yolk -- similar to above; fried in sweet syrup

tong yib ทองหยิบ

egg yolk -- similar to above

kaao niaw moon ข้าวเหนียวมูล

sticky rice -- together with different sweets and fruits available, see following examples:

kaao niaw mamuang ข้าวเหนียวมะม่วง

sticky rice -- served with fresh mangos and coconut cream

kaao niaw turian ข้าวเหนียวทุเรียน

sticky rice -- served with a cream of durian and coconut milk

kaao niaw sang kayaa ข้าวเหนียวสังขยา

sticky rice -- served with pudding and coconut cream

kaao lam ข้าวหลาม

sticky rice -- with coconut cream and black beans in the bamboo stick *kaao tom mat* ข้าวต้มมัด

sticky rice -- in palm leaves with bananas and black beans

kluai buat chee กล้วยบวดชี

bananas -- served in sweet coconut milk

kluai kaek กล้วยแขก

bananas -- fried

kluai chueam กล้วยเชื่อม

bananas -- backed in sweet syrup

look taan chueam ลูกตาลเชื่อม

palm heart -- in sweet syrup

look chup ลูกชุบ

candy -- beans with jelly glaze

ta go ตะโก้

candy -- in palm leaves with coconut cream

kanom bueang ขนมเบื้อง

biscuit, cookie -- with egg yolk and coconut cream or salty with onions

sarim ซาหริ่ม

candy noodles -- with sugar peas, coconut milk and crushed ice

lot chong ลอดช่อง

jelly noodles -- similar to *'sarim'*; green in colour

At the restaurant

A table for two, please.

To samrap song khon.
โต๊ะสำหรับสองคน

I am expecting some friends.

Phom gamlang raw phuean.
ผมกำลังรอเพื่อน

Please bring me ...

Garuna aw ...
กรุณาเอา...

Can I see the menu.

Kho menyu nooi khrap.
ขอเมนูหน่อยครับ

I did not order this.

Phom mai daai sang chaan nee.
ผมไม่ได้สั่งจานนี้

Did you order already ?

Sang laew rue yung khrap ?
สั่งแล้วหรือยังครับ

I am hungry.

Hiw kaao.
หิวข้าว

I did not eat yet.

Phom yung mai daai thaan kaao.
ผมยังไม่ได้ทานข้าว

What would you like to eat ?

Khun yaak thaan arai ?
คุณอยากทานอะไร

Is the food ready ?

Aahaan set laew rue yung ?
อาหารเสร็จแล้วหรือยัง

Ready !

Set laew khrap !
เสร็จแล้วครับ

Would you like to taste ?

Chim nooi mai ?
ชิมหน่อยไหม

That looks delicious.

Doo naa thaan.
ดูน่าทาน

That smells delicious.

Hom naa thaan.
หอมน่าทาน

Delicious ?

Arooi mai ?
อร่อยไหม

Very delicious.

Arooi maak.
อร่อยมาก

Would you like some more ?

Thaan arai eek mai ?
ทานอะไรอีกไหม

Are you still hungry ?

Im laew rue yung ?
อิ่มแล้วหรือยัง

I am full.

Im laew.
อิ่มแล้ว

Pay, please ! The bill, please !

Kep ngoen duai ! Chek bin duai !
เก็บเงินด้วย/ เช็คบิลด้วย

At the bar

I am thirsty.

Hiw naam.
หิวน้ำ

I have a very try throat.

Kho haeng.
คอแห้ง

What would you like to drink ?

Khun tawng gaan duem arai ?
คุณต้องการดื่มอะไร

I want to drink beer.

Yaak duem bia.
อยากดื่มเบียร์

Let's drink a beer.

Duem bia na.
ดื่มเบียร์นะ

Would you like to drink some more ?

Khun tawng gaan duem arai eek mai ?
คุณต้องการดื่มอะไรอีกไหม

Drink some more !

Duem eek nooi see !
ดื่มอีกหน่อยสิ

Cheers!

Chon gaew !
ชนแก้ว

You can drink !

Duem keng chaang.
ดื่มเก่งจัง

How much did you drink already ?

Khun duem kee gaew laew ?
คุณดื่มกี่แก้วแล้ว

Are you drunk ?

Mao laew rue yung ?
เมาแล้วหรือยัง

I want more !

Aw eek !
เอาอีก

Didn't you drink a little bit too much ?

Mao maak pai rue plaao ?
เมามากไปหรือเปล่า

You better stop drinking now.

Naa cha yut duem daai laew.
น่าจะหยุดดื่มได้แล้ว

We better go home now !

Glup baan dee kwaa !
กลับบ้านดีกว่า

Good Night.

Latisawat
ราตรีสวัสด์

English - Thai - All you have to know

Available as pocket book

P a p e r b a c k

Index

Please note: **bold** numbers refer to useful phrases and examples

C

Please note: **bold** numbers refer to useful phrases and examples

Please note: **bold** numbers refer to useful phrases and examples

Please note: **bold** numbers refer to useful phrases and examples

M

Please note: **bold** numbers refer to useful phrases and examples

Please note: **bold** numbers refer to useful phrases and examples

Please note: **bold** numbers refer to useful phrases and examples

U

V

W

Please note: **bold** numbers refer to useful phrases and examples

Check out our other books !

Available everywhere in Thailand or order online at

www.hotspicy.co.th